SUNJATA

A New Prose Version

SUNJATA

A New Prose Version

Edited and Translated,
with an Introduction, by
David C. Conrad

Hackett Publishing Company, Inc.
Indianapolis/Cambridge

19 18 17 16   1 2 3 4 5 6 7

For further information, please address
   Hackett Publishing Company, Inc.
   P.O. Box 44937
   Indianapolis, Indiana 46244-0937

   www.hackettpublishing.com

Cover design by Rick Todhunter
Interior design by Elizabeth L. Wilson
Composition by Aptara, Inc.

Library of Congress Cataloging-in-Publication Data
Names: Conrad, David C., editor, translator. | Condé,
   Djanka Tassey, storyteller.
Title: Sunjata : a new prose version / edited and translated, with an
   introduction, by David C. Conrad.
Description: Indianapolis : Hackett Publishing Company, 2016. |
   Translated from Mandingo. | Based on a performance by
   Djanka Tassey Condâe.
Identifiers: LCCN 2016002415| ISBN 9781624664946 (pbk.) |
   ISBN 9781624664953 (cloth)
Subjects: LCSH: Keita, Soundiata, –1255—Legends. | Mandingo
   (African people)—Folklore. | Legends—Mali. | Mali (Empire)—
   Folklore.
Classification: LCC GR352.82.M34 S86 2016 | DDC 398.208996345—dc23
LC record available at http://lccn.loc.gov/2016002415

This book is dedicated to my friend and colleague

Djibril Tamsir Niane

who introduced the Sunjata epic to the non-Mande world with the first widely circulated prose version and who, with the Condé jeliw *of Fadama, is the* sabu *of this work*

And to the memory of my friend and teacher

Fadama Babou Condé

d. 28/2/2016

CONTENTS

ACKNOWLEDGMENTS

The research in Guinea that produced the material for this book was funded by a Fulbright Senior Research Grant administered by the Council for the International Exchange of Scholars, African Regional Research Program.

My work with the Condé bards of Fadama, Guinea, was facilitated by Djibril Tamsir Niane, who provided me with a written introduction early in 1994 that led to everything accomplished since then through my relationship with the Condé and associated Kouyaté bards, most of whom are now deceased.

During a period of many months of 1994 in Kissidougou, Guinea, Djobba Kamara and Lansana Magassouba labored with me to extract the oral discourse from the original tape recordings, producing rough word-for-word translation that enabled me to render the oral narrative into its present form. The work was accomplished in a space graciously provided by Ms. Keri Giller, then of the U.S. Peace Corps.

To Kassim Koné I owe a great debt of gratitude for his explanations of complicated family relationships, indigenous cuisine and other esoteric cultural matters.

I want to express my deep appreciation to Rick Todhunter of Hackett Publishing Company for his work on the prose version, and for his patience during the long wait for me to find time for this project.

INTRODUCTION

The Cultural and Historical Context

The great African epic that is popularly known by the name of its central hero Sunjata is an essential part of the fabric of Mande culture. The heartland of Mande territory is located in what is now northeastern Guinea and southern Mali, but the Mande peoples are found in a much larger portion of sub-Saharan West Africa, speaking various related languages and dialects of the Mande family of languages.

Mande peoples are heirs to an extremely rich and vibrant historical legacy, the high point of which was the Mali Empire that flourished from roughly the mid-13th to the early-15th century CE. The epic narrative of Sunjata and his contemporaries illustrates the Mande peoples' own view of the glorious past, and it rightfully credits their ancestors with establishing one of the great empires of the medieval world.

Among the related peoples of Manding culture, oral tradition is the domain of bards popularly known as "griots" but as *jeliw* or *jelilu* (sing. *jeli*) to their own people. They are the hereditary oral artists responsible for maintaining the lively oral discourse that recalls the alleged deeds of the early ancestors, keeping them and their exploits alive in the community's collective memory. The *jeliw* are born into an occupationally defined group of oral artists and craft specialists whose families customarily intermarry with one another, thereby helping to preserve monopolies on the areas of interest that account for their livelihood. For many centuries the *jeliw* have served as genealogists, musicians, praise-singers, spokespersons, and diplomats. As the principal narrators of oral tradition, the bards have been responsible for preserving narratives that express what peoples of the Mande cultural heartland believe to have happened in the distant past. Stories of the ancestors were passed from one generation of *jeliw* to the next down through the centuries, and the principal Manding clans frame their own identities in terms of descent from the ancestors of epic tradition.

As specialists in maintaining the oral traditions of their culture, *jeliw* are known to their own people as guardians of "The Word." In early times they served as the spokespersons of chiefs (*dugutigiw*) and kings (*mansaw*), and were thus responsible for their patrons' reputations in the community. Generations of *jeli* families were permanently attached to the leading households and ruling dynasties, from whom the bards received everything they required to support their families in exchange for their services in the oral arts. The *jeliw* fulfilled these responsibilities with praise-songs and narratives describing the great deeds of their patrons' ancestors. As advisers to distinguished personages, bards encouraged their patrons to achieve high goals by reminding them of the examples set by their heroic ancestors as described in the epic narratives. The *jeliw* would point out mistakes through the use of proverbs, and admonish their patrons when they threatened to fail in their duties. At the same time, the bards' own security depended on their rulers' political power and social prestige, so the stories they told tended to be biased in favor of their own patrons' ancestors at the expense of their rivals and enemies. This, among many other factors, doubtless contributed to distortion in the oral tradition, which is why many scholars refuse to take them seriously as sources of historical evidence.

While Manding peoples depend on their *jeliw* and the epic narratives for their perceptions of what happened in the distant past, many scholars from outside Manding society do not believe oral tradition is a useful source of historical information. Indeed, some have expressed disbelief that Sunjata ever really existed. This has been a fundamental difference between the local African point of view and the perspectives of some foreign academics. All things considered, the Mande oral epic demands our attention because it provides otherwise inaccessible information about this people's world view. But regardless of what other options arguably exist, it would be lamentably shortsighted to ignore the voices of Manding peoples themselves. The subjects that the *jeliw* favor as being of historical interest are representative of Manding cultural values. They are presented with consummate artistry and engaging perspectives that are expressed in one of the world's great epic narratives, and they provide richly textured insights into what one West African society feels is important in its distant past.

The Manding peoples' ideas of what is most important in the past are markedly different from the kinds of history that are studied and appreciated by people strictly adhering to European standards of scholarship. For one thing, in Manding societies all matters involving family, clan, and ethnic kinship are of supreme importance. People are identified by their *jamu*, which is the family name or patronymic associated with one or more famous ancestors who are remembered for important deeds that are alleged to have occurred around the beginning of the 13th century. Today, thanks to regular exposure to live or locally taped performances by *jeliw* that are played privately or heard regularly on local radio broadcasts, general awareness of the heroes and heroines of ancient times enters the people's consciousness in childhood and remains there throughout their lives. Memories of the ancestors are constantly evoked in praise-songs and narrative episodes that are sung or recited by the bards on virtually any occasion that calls for entertainment. In the elaborate greetings that are tendered during social encounters, friends, acquaintances, and strangers alike salute each other with reference to their respective *jamuw*, that is to, say family names that extend back to distinguished ancestors of the heroic past. When strangers meet, they quickly learn each other's *jamuw* or patronymics, thus establishing their relative places in the cultural landscape. Travelers meeting far from home soon establish relationships through their *jamuw*, because of links that are believed to have formed between their ancestors during encounters that are described in the epic narrative. Strangers arriving in distant towns or villages establish immediate connections with "related" families and find comfort and security with their hosts. When elders meet in village council, the ancestral spirits are felt to be present, because according to tradition, it was they who established the relative statuses of everyone present, as well as the administrative protocols to be followed and the values underpinning every decision. It is no exaggeration to say that regardless of gender, the ancestors who are described in *kuma koro* or "ancient speech" define the identity of virtually everyone of Manding origin.

Out of Fadama: The Life and Perspectives of a Mande Bard

Djanka Tassey Condé, the *jeli* on whose performance of the Sunjata epic this translation is based, lived his entire life in the small village of Fadama near the Niandan River in northeastern Guinea. For most of his adult life he lived in the shadow of his brother Djanka Mamadi, who, like Tassey, was identified by the name of their mother, Djanka. Their father, Babu Condé (d. 1964), was one of the most famous bards of the colonial era, when Guinea was part of French West Africa. Babu was descended from a lineage of Condé bards who trace their ancestry to forebears who lived in the land of Dò ni Kiri, as it is described in the Mande epic. Even among other bardic families of Manden, the Condé of Fadama are respected for their vast knowledge of Mande epic tradition. In the 1970s and '80s when Mamadi Condé was *belentigi* (chief bard) of Fadama, he was one of the best-known orators in Manden, distinguished for the depth of knowledge that he displayed in his epic discourse. When Mamadi died in 1994, his brother Tassey became the *belentigi*. Several months later in that same year, the editor of this book arrived in Fadama to begin a collaborative relationship with Tassey Condé that lasted until that great bard's death in 1997.

Many *jeliw* accompany themselves on indigenous musical instruments such as the *nkoni* (a small lute), the *kora* (a twenty-one string calabash harp), or the *bala* (a native xylophone). Others recite their narratives accompanied by *naamu*-sayers, and this was how Tassey performed in his home village. When we were in Tassey's house recording the performance on which this translation is based, there were two or three *naamu*-sayers who took turns accompanying the bard during the course of each performance. A *naamu*-sayer or responding person is a secondary performer whose job it is to reply to and encourage the main performer with short interjected comments. The most common interjection is *naamu*, for which there is no very accurate translation, though it is what people also say when they hear their name called, and it can be rendered as "yes," or "I hear you." Among other expressions commonly heard from encouragers are *tinye* (it's true"), *walahi* ("I swear"), and *amina* ("amen"), which is usually heard after a spoken blessing. Occasionally, when the encourager is especially excited by something the bard says, he will repeat the line or interject a comment of several words (see pg. 131, the glossary entry "naamu"). The words of the *naamu*-sayers were an important part of Tassey Condé's performance, but for ease of reading they have been omitted from the present prose translation.[1] The bard's own comments and asides are similarly important to the performance, and I've retained them here for textual authenticity and for the insights they provide into Mande culture. (They are also quite entertaining and often humorous.) The recording sessions took place inside a small, circular, thatch-roofed house. The bard sat on the floor with his *naamu*-sayers and a small, intimate audience, and it would be helpful for readers to imagine themselves seated among them on goatskins and grass mats with their backs against the mud-brick wall.

---

1. The interjections of the *naamu*-sayers are reproduced in my more literal verse translation, published by Hackett in 2004.

The *jeliw* who tell the stories of the ancestors in the time of Sunjata think of the language employed on those occasions as *kuma koro* ("ancient speech"). Musical performances involving the singing of stories and praises about Sunjata are called *Sunjata fasaw*, and the overall narrative is known as Manden *maana*, or Manden *tariku*. It consists of a series of episodes that comprise a core narrative known by virtually any *jeli* performer. Details vary from one bard to the next, but the core episodes follow more or less the same basic outline no matter who tells it. Nevertheless, some *jeliw* are more knowledgeable than others, and a few, as in the case of Tassey Condé, provide details or even entire episodes that are not heard from other performers. In the best-known episodes as told by some bards, a particular character behaves in some odd, seemingly inexplicable way, or strange things happen for no apparent reason. For example, some *jeliw* describe how Dò Kamissa the Buffalo Woman gives away the secret of how she can be killed, without providing any explanation of why she would do so. Similarly, descriptions of the pregnancy of Sunjata's mother seem entirely mythological, owing to claims that it dragged on for seven years. In the present version, Tassey Condé provides reasonable motives and logical explanations for these and other elements that would previously be consigned to the realm of pure fantasy.

Through dozens of generations of storytelling, bards have doubtless forgotten much of the earliest discourse, distorted surviving parts, and created new elements, so it is extremely difficult to know for sure what, if any, genuinely historical facts might have survived in reference to people and events of the Mali Empire. Tassey Condé's versions of the core episodes are presented in this book, along with a few less common episodes that are of particular interest. Parts of the general outline of the story of Sunjata and other epic heroes and heroines are more or less familiar to most ordinary citizens of traditional Manding societies, which is one of the characteristics that qualify it as an epic. Owing to what Manding peoples are repeatedly told by the *jeliw*, they think of the characters in the epic as their own ancestors, and those epic heroes and heroines serve as examples for ideal behavior.

Individual episodes of the Sunjata narrative highlight various themes that demonstrate the values and ideals of the society from which the epic evolved through many generations of professional storytellers. Tassey Condé reflects the Manding peoples' interest in questions of political power and authority early in his version of the epic, by listing seven kings (*mansaw*) who ruled autonomous chiefdoms prior to the time when Manden was unified into a single great state of the Western Sudan. In all versions of the epic, Sunjata Keita is the hero consistently acknowledged as the leader who liberates Manden from Soso oppression and becomes *mansa* of the unified chiefdoms (*jamanaw*) that subsequently expand into the Mali Empire. For that reason, in today's Manding societies the Keita *jamu* carries special distinction, even for those not directly connected to village chiefs whose claims to authority are based on alleged descent from Sunjata's lineage. However, at performances by modern-day *jeliw*, members of many other families bask in the reflected glory of early kings, because Tassey Condé and other particularly knowledgeable bards identify various numbers of *mansaw* who ruled individual *jamanaw* in Manden during the period leading up to imperial unification. The *jeliw* do not always list the same *mansaw*, so all told there may be as many as a dozen charismatic leaders who are actually named, thus effectively increasing the opportunities for reflected glory available to their alleged descendants in latter-day audiences.

Extended Kinship and Supernatural Powers: Ancestors Who Shaped the Mande World

Some of the Maninka bards, including Tassey Condé, refer to Sumaworo Kanté of Soso as one of the "original" *mansaw* of Manden. A popular image has emerged of the Soso ruler as little more than a bloodthirsty "evil demon." This is traceable to a widely read novelette, D. T. Niane's *Sundiata* (1965), which was based on one version of the epic narrative. That book stresses Sumaworo's brutality with his beheading of enemies and his shoes made of human skin. This conveys a false impression of how Sumaworo is actually perceived, because it fails to reveal that the alleged brutality is only one aspect of a multidimensional character portrayed by the Manding *jeliw*. Like other bards, Tassey Condé embellishes Sumaworo's reputation as a great sorcerer king through the attribution of appropriately terrifying deeds, including the wearing of human-skin apparel (p. 116), but he also credits him with being the provider of a great cultural legacy of fine musical instruments (p. 60). Sumaworo is described as eventually seizing control of Manden and ruling as a tyrant, but at the same time he is perceived as having been one of the seven *mansaw* who laid the groundwork for one of the great civilizations of West Africa (p. 98). Indeed, had Sunjata and the armies of Manden not succeeded in bringing an end to Sumaworo's ambitions, the latter's southward expansion to incorporate the Mande *jamanaw* into Soso might have eventually led to an empire similar in scope to the one that emerged as Mali.

The earliest episodes of the epic are concerned with the hardships involved in conceiving the hero that will launch the Mali Empire. In accord with the Manding systems of belief, the quest for future glory is set in motion by diviners who foresee the coming of a hero and prescribe the steps needed to achieve the prophesied outcome. Sunjata's father, Maghan Konfara, is a relatively minor character whose problems as related by the *jeliw* do not compare to the severe hardships suffered by his female counterpart, Sogolon Condé. The father's problems consist of a series of frustrating failures to produce children with various wives as he follows the instructions of his diviners, who are trying to identify the woman destined to be Sunjata's mother. In Manding oral tradition, everything involved in the conception of a hero of Sunjata's stature is normally characterized by hardships endured by both mother and son that set the hero apart from the rest of society. In the performance of a gifted bard like Tassey

Condé, key phrases can succinctly define fundamental Manding values. Speaking of the father's difficulties in locating the future mother, the bard says, "It's hard to give birth to a child who will be famous!" (p. 11). Once the correct woman is found and impregnated, Maghan Konfara recedes into the background, and in most versions of the epic the specific occasion of his death goes unnoticed. Quite the opposite is true of Sogolon Condé, who continues as a central figure in several episodes. She is gradually revealed to be one of the great heroines of Manding oral traditions, and her death is invariably noted as a significant event in the narrative.

In Manding epic traditions, the greatest heroes do not acquire their special powers from their fathers. It is the mothers who are perceived as the sources (*sabuw*) of their sons' greatness, and these women invariably suffer severe hardships before the hero is born. Such adversity is part of the formula for the future glory of a leader who initiates momentous change in the lives of his people. Sogolon Condé is the source of Sunjata's greatness, so the quest to locate her, and descriptions of her trials and tribulations, take up several episodes of the epic. In her first appearance, Sogolon is the forgotten girl of her village, bypassed for years by all suitors because she is too ugly to marry. When the Buffalo Woman reveals certain secrets, we learn how Sogolon acquired her physical deformities. The hunters who select Sogolon according to their pact with the Buffalo Woman, subsequently try to abandon her. Later, once Sogolon is pregnant, her rival co-wives cause her to suffer repeated miscarriages for several years before she can succeed in the painful and potentially life-threatening process of giving birth, or what the Bamana describe as "women's war." When the long-awaited hero is finally born, Sogolon suffers the anguish of coping with her son's lameness as well as additional abuse from her co-wives. As the narrator Tassey Condé remarks, "It's said that greatness will not be acquired without hardship" (p. 33).

According to values that are often reaffirmed in the general corpus of Manding oral traditions, it is imperative that Sunjata's iron resolve and other leadership qualities be forged on the anvil of both his and his mother's sufferings. In the mother's case, those ordeals comprise only one dimension of Sogolon's character. Many of the most important women in Manding oral traditions are described as sorceresses, and Sogolon is one of the most powerful of these. Sorcery, or the manipulation of occult power (*dalilu*), is an important part of a shared Manding cosmology. That belief system involves complex strategies for communicating with the supernatural world through sacrifice, masked ritual, incantation, divination, and healing with various kinds of medicine (*basi*), including herbs, powders, potions, and amulets. It also includes personal interaction with various kinds of spirits that dwell in bodies of water, in caves and large rock formations, and in forest groves. The spirits have individual identities and archaic, pre-Islamic terms to describe them, but in general they are simply referred to as *jinn* (genies), a word borrowed from Islamic tradition.

In Sogolon's case, it is her *dalilu* or powers of sorcery that enable her to survive and to meet the series of challenges that mark her own path to greatness. Before delivering Sogolon to her future husband, the hunters each attempt to have sex with her and are pierced by porcupine quills, or (in some versions) mauled as if they were trying to molest a lioness (p. 38). Wounded and humiliated, the brothers try to abandon Sogolon, but find her waiting when they arrive at their destination (p. 40). Sogolon's initial encounter with her husband Maghan Konfara, is characterized by a fierce sorcerer's contest in which she severely tests the defenses of Sunjata's future father. But if Sogolon's occult powers see her through various difficulties and establish her credentials as the mother of a hero, they also initiate trouble. During her marriage celebration she reveals her formidable powers to her co-wives who are also sorceresses (p. 43), and this sets off their deadly rivalry: "they dipped their hands into their *dalilu*" (p. 47).

If the *jeliw* recall Sogolon Condé and her co-wives as having formidable powers of sorcery, the same can be said of many other—though not all—female ancestors mentioned by name in the Sunjata epic. Mande epic discourse revels in the power of women in general, expressed on one level through their command of metaphysical processes like sorcery, but also through heroines whose resources are limited to personal courage and traditional areas of female influence. In other words, some women of the Sunjata epic such as Fakoli's wife Keleya Konkon and Sunjata's sister Kolonkan achieve notable deeds using sorcery, while others like Sumaworo's sister Kosiya Kanté distinguish themselves through their own natural courage and abilities.

Identifying archetypal figures of the distant past as masters of supernatural power is the bard's way of accounting for the ancestors' momentous contributions to Mande civilization. Availing himself of poetic license, the Maninka oral artist paints with a vocal brush on a broad canvas of colorful sound, producing larger-than-life heroes and heroines. Thus imprinted on the collective Manding consciousness, key ancestors who represent each of the principal families achieve the status of cultural icons, establishing legacies that their descendants can be proud of. According to the social ideal as conveyed in *jeli* performances, latter-day descendants should seek to emulate their illustrious forebears.

In addition to Sogolon, some of the most prominent female sorcerers include Sogolon's formidable elder sister Kamissa of Dò. Transforming herself into a man-killing buffalo (p. 18), Kamissa launches a series of events climaxed by her self-induced death (p. 32), thus facilitating Sogolon's introduction to Sunjata's future father. Sunjata's sister Kolonkan calls on her own *dalilu* when needed, as she does when seeking meat for the delegation that arrives to take Sunjata back to Manden. On that occasion Kolonkan removes the hearts and livers of wild game killed by her brothers without leaving a mark on the carcasses (p. 83). At first glance, women's feats of magic often seem to be limited to traditional domestic duties, but the political significance of their exploits should not be overlooked. Kolonkan's ritual hospitality to the search party from Manden heralds the impending return of her brother Sunjata to release his people from their bondage to

Soso and establish the foundations of the Mali Empire. Simi-larly, when Fakoli's wife Keleya Konkon prepares hundreds of helpings of a half-dozen different meals simultaneously in a single cooking pot (p. 106), she is a central participant in sacrificial feasting as a prelude to war and is subsequently detained as a political hostage. When Fakoli's mother Kosiya Kanté sacrifices herself to the genies so her brother Suma-woro can acquire the occult objects that he craves (p. 70), she enhances her son's mystique as the blacksmith-sorcerer ancestor, and opens the path to her brother's power as *mansa* of the Soso Kingdom. Kosiya's co-wife Tenenba Condé assumes the outwardly mundane domestic responsibility of becoming Fakoli's foster mother (p. 73). However, as one of the three great Condé sisters of Dò ni Kiri, Tenenba is a sor-ceress in her own right, and it is she who sees to it that Fakoli acquires the protective devices and spiritual power that will account for his legendary presence at the vortex of the Mand-ing power structure (p. 74).

The heroic male ancestors are similarly endowed with occult powers by the *jeliw* who maintain the charismatic ancestors in a shared Manding consciousness. Magic among the ancestors is often associated with hunters and warriors who require supernatural gifts to survive their encounters with dangerous animals and deadly enemies. In the final episode of this book, the enemy king Jolofin Mansa trans-forms himself into a crocodile to escape Sunjata's soldiers (p. 124), but Sitafa Diawara has the *dalilu* required to prevail over the beast after being swallowed by it (p. 126). As a sur-viving contemporary of Sunjata's father, Kamanjan Kamara of Sibi is a link to an earlier generation of sorcerer kings. When Sunjata pays his respects to the Sibi *mansa*, Kamanjan warns the young hero that he will need all his *dalilu* to battle Sumaworo of Soso, making his point by causing a large tree to flip upside down onto its top branches (p. 112). Sunjata occasionally demonstrates his own occult powers, as when he employs magic during the river-crossing with his mother and siblings (p. 89), and he matches the tree-flipping magic of Kamanjan of Sibi (p. 112). However, sorcery is less central to

Sunjata's image and accomplishments than it is to Sumaworo Kanté, the *mansa* of Soso. In Sumaworo's youth he negotiates with forest genies to acquire objects that form the basis of his occult powers (p. 64). As *mansa* of Soso, Sumaworo emerges as one of the great sorcerers of Manding epic, with abilities that are enhanced by a private oracle, Nènèba, which unerringly identifies future threats to its master's political power (p. 78).

If the indigenous system of belief, with its sorcery, sacred sites, initiation societies, medicines, masks, and arcane ritual, is the spiritual backbone of Manding epic tradition, Islam also plays a major role in the events described. Islam had arrived in parts of sub-Saharan West Africa long before the 13th-century events described in the Sunjata epic, but the extent of its influence on Manding society by that time is extremely difficult to determine. For commercial and political reasons, some rulers and prosperous traders are known to have become at least nominally Muslim by the 11th century: the kingdoms of Takrur, Ghana/Wagadu, and Gao all had resident Muslim merchants by at least 1000 to 1100 CE, and a chief of the Juddala tribe of the Sanhaja of the western Sahara went on the pilgrimage to Mecca in 1035. As for the Mali Empire, Sunjata's own son Mansa Wali made the pilgrimage during the time of Sultan Zubayr of Egypt sometime between 1260 and 1277.

Despite some early conversions in sub-Saharan West Africa, the vast bulk of the Manding population did not become Muslim. Indeed, in the earliest instances, many of those who did profess Islam most likely did not entirely abandon their traditional system of belief, and the same is true in modern times. Manding villagers were basically interested in maintaining any connections with the spirit world that would provide them with health and well-being at the very least, and prosperity at best. From the earliest days of Islam's appearance among sub-Saharan black African societies like the Manding, certain elements of Islam—such as praying in the direction of Mecca—that appeared likely to contribute to individual or community well-being would be adopted into the local system of belief. Moreover, any sort of link with the Holy Lands of Arabia came to be regarded as an important source of blessings and prestige. West African chiefs and kings began making the pilgrimage to Mecca as early as the 11th century, thereby affirming—and enhancing—their power and authority. Other sectors of Manding society were provided with imaginary links to Mecca and the Prophet Muhammad when the bards appropriated heroes from Arabic tradition and claimed them as ancestors. For example, the legendary first *muezzin* or "caller to prayers" in Mecca was a big-voiced black African former slave named Surakata whom the *jeliw* claim was their ancestor. In oral tradition, Muslim *moriw* are diviners who are frequently consulted for their wisdom. The best example from the Sunjata epic is that the primary identity of one of the central characters, Manjan Bereté, is "the first Muslim leader of Manden" and an influential adviser to Sunjata's father (p. 11).

However, such acknowledgment of the power and prestige of Islam did not mean abandoning the ancient water and earth spirits of the pre-Islamic ancestors. Attractive elements of the Middle Eastern religion were appropriated and claimed as part of the indigenous system of belief, thus establishing a combined religion in a process called syncretism. In Manding tradition this is dramatically expressed by a pilgrimage legend in which the hero Fajigi goes to Mecca, acquires the traditional sacrificial (pre-Islamic) objects including masks and altars, and returns with them to Manden. Thus, by claiming that a number of distinguished ancestors originated in Arabia during the time of the Prophet Muhammad (p. 20), and with the similarly dramatic claim that the paraphernalia of traditional spirit ritual originated in Mecca, the *jeliw* provided links between Mecca and Manding villagers who could only dream of making the pilgrimage themselves. The presence of these existential values in the Manding system of belief are found in Tassey Condé's frequent references to traditional notions of occult powers like *dalilu*, *dabali*, and the arts of divination. Members of Tassey's audience probably attend Friday prayers at the village mosque, but they see no contradiction in continuing to take seriously the ancient rituals, sacred places, and forest spirits described in the Sunjata story.

While the *jeliw* attribute formidable occult powers to many legendary ancestors of both genders, it is Fakoli Koroma who sets the standard for sorcery among those charismatic leaders of early times. In the epic tradition, Fakoli is still a child on his foster mother's back when he is carried to a series of important sacred sites and introduced to the principal rulers of the Mande territories (p. 69). During the course of this journey the infant acquires a wealth of protective medicines, blessings, and amulets that are necessary for his future life as one of the greatest battle commanders of his era, as the most powerful of sorcerers, and as the legendary patriarch of several blacksmith clans. The *jeliw* consistently portray the adult Fakoli as being dwarflike in stature, and the praise songs refer to him as "Big-headed, big-mouthed Fakoli." When Fakoli marches to war he wears a medicine bonnet adorned with an array of potent objects, including dried birds' heads, horns, and amulets. The most famous occasion on which Fakoli reveals his enormous powers is a meeting among the elders, when this shortest of heroes bends low to pass through the council hall doorway that towers high over his head. Fakoli is ridiculed for this seemingly absurd pretense, but replies by demonstrating that a man's true size is not always readily visible. He temporarily enlarges himself to such a size that he raises the roof of the council hall (in some versions he wears it like a hat), and the men who ridiculed him are squeezed against the walls by his magically expanded bulk (p. 101).

The ancestors' ongoing involvement with sorcery, divination, ritual sacrifice, and genies vividly reflects the Manding peoples' pervasive interest in the supernatural world, but that drama plays out in the natural world of human relationships. Where the temporal world is concerned, the *jeliw* like to describe how families, clans, and chiefdoms interacted with one another in ancient times. Local audiences find these descriptions to be intensely interesting, because in some cases they influence their own relationships with people in today's world. In the "joking relationships" called *senankuya,* a member of one family will humorously insult someone of another family because of something alleged to have happened between their ancestors. For example, when men of the Condé and Traoré clans meet for the first time, one will jokingly claim that the other is his slave, and the other will argue that the reverse is true.

As portrayed by *jeli* discourse, the relationships between key ancestral figures had far deeper significance than what is suggested by joking insults. Readers should keep in mind that the colorful, larger-than-life characters who orbit around Sunjata are participants in events that lead to the founding of the Mali Empire. In the process, the charismatic ancestors contribute to the establishment of a social framework kept so alive and vibrant by the *jeliw*, that it has endured to modern times. According to the bards, many of the most important families of ancient times were somehow related to one another through marriage, and those liaisons still contribute to the prestige of families in contemporary Manding societies. Similarly, to whatever extent interested parties of today are conscious of legendary details (their numbers decline with every passing generation), memorable encounters between non-blood-bound ancestral lineages can influence joking relationships between friends and political or business competitors. Tassey Condé explains Faran Tunkara's refusal to provide land for Sogolon's burial as an excuse to quarrel with Sunjata and retain him as leader of his army (p. 91). As in the unusual instance noted above where Kamissa reveals the secret of how the buffalo can be killed, most versions of the epic do not include a reason for Tunkara's refusal of a burial plot, nor do they allow the king of Nema to cleverly extricate himself from difficulty by claiming a protocol was violated, thus denying him the privilege of honoring Sogolon (p. 93).

According to the reservoir of knowledge preserved by many generations of the Condé family of Fadama and passed down to Djanka Tassey, Sunjata was related, either directly or by marriage, to an astonishing number of other major characters in the Mande epic. Some of the family relationships are standard elements of the epic while others are less often seen.

Concerns with the relationships between Sunjata, Fakoli, Sumaworo, Turama'an, Kamanjan, the Condé sisters of Dò ni Kiri, and all the other major characters are present in most versions of the epic regardless of who tells the story, and the importance of kinship, social intrigue, and political alliance is central to the spirit of the oral tradition. Individual narrators, following on earlier generations of family members who taught them their art, sometimes contribute unusual features to their versions, and this is true of the Fadama pool of knowledge from which our text is drawn. In Tassey Condé's version there are other, less prominent faces in the exquisitely detailed crowd of characters who populate this epic panorama, contributing socially integrated additions to the great family web of which Sunjata is the center. During Maghan Konfara's search for the woman who will give birth to the child of heroic destiny, his diviners tap into various segments of the female population. They advise him to marry a light-skinned woman, so he marries nine of them, but none deliver the child in question. This process is repeated in turn with nine each of mulatto women, black women, slave girls, and female bards. Regarding the references to skin color, one of the Maninka terms is translated as "light-skinned" and another is "mulatto," because Manding social consciousness recognizes a variety of light and dark skin shades ranging from "white" to "yellow" and "red" (e.g., one of the standard names for Sunjata's mother is Sogolon Wulen, or "Red Sogolon"). Along with slave girls and female bards, the various female "types" and their exaggerated numbers are employed by the raconteur to dramatize the extraordinary efforts made to identify the future queen mother foreseen by the diviners.

In each case, when the bard announces that the desired child was not produced, he inserts a subtle contradiction by specifically naming one of the women to the effect that "But aside from Marabajan Tarawelé, none of those mulatto women gave birth," or "But aside from Nyuma Damba Magasuba, none of them bore any children" (p. 10). The easily overlooked "aside from" remarks convey the notion that other children resulted from the marriages to different groups of females. Thus, in this version of the story, the number and identity of Sunjata's half-siblings is augmented to include representatives of a wide spectrum of the social order, including a slave and a female bard (p. 10).

Such liberal alleged integration into the royal bloodline could be interpreted to indicate a belief on the narrator's part that there were no social boundaries in the time of Maghan Konfara, and that a *mansa* would marry a slave or a female bard. The question of when class and occupational distinctions became part of Manding social organization is of great interest to scholars, and despite the risks of relying on oral tradition for historical information, they are interested in what it has to say on the subject. In this case, it seems most likely that the bard is merely embellishing his story and enhancing the prestige of Sunjata's father. Regarding the first group of women, he says Maghan Konfara married nine of them "because of his power" (p. 10). Such things are subject to various interpretations by non-Manding outsiders, according to their individual literary, cultural, or historical interests. For present purposes, it is sufficient to note that in celebratory performances commissioned by prosperous community leaders of Manding towns and villages, the bards' descriptions of far-reaching family alliances contribute to the audiences' sense of their own connections to great people of the distant past. People named Bereté, Condé, Diabaté, Diawara, Kamara, Keita, Koroma, Kouyaté, Kulubali, Magasuba, Traoré, and many others take pride in the distinguished ancestors of the same name, while awareness of those legendary people's specific relationships to Sunjata contributes to a general sense of political and cultural unity.

Stories of co-wife and sibling rivalry, such as the drama that plays out between Sogolon and Sunjata versus Sansun Berete and Dankaran Tuman, repeatedly highlight family strife as a favorite subject in Manding oral traditions. One of the most enduring consequences of family conflict pits sister against brother in an episode where Kolonkan seizes the initiative in a politically sensitive situation and exploits her social position as hostess to the extremely important delegation from Manden. Finding herself with no meat in the house, Kolonkan goes into the bush and, using her *dalilu*, extracts the hearts and livers of wild game killed by her brothers (p. 83). When the hunters retrieve their kill, Manden Bori is furious, because he thinks Kolonkan is disrespecting her brothers and showing off for the guests by unnecessarily exercising her sorcery. In full view of the delegates from Manden, he chases Kolonkan and causes her wrapper to come off (p. 85). Despite a social convention that sisters are expected to have great influence over the fate of their brothers, Manden Bori further humiliates Kolonkan by using his own sorcery to cause fresh blood to flow from the meat that his sister had cooked for their guests. Kolonkan accuses Manden Bori of shaming her in front of the Mande people whom she was entertaining according to her customary duties and for the family benefit. She then places a curse on Manden Bori and his branch of the Keita royal lineage, declaring that the *mansaya* (kingship) would be passed down to them, but that they would never peacefully agree on who would hold the power (p. 90). There is reasonably reliable evidence in the Arabic writings of Ibn Khaldun that historically the *mansaya* did pass from the line of Sunjata to that of his brother. Manden Bori's descendants are said to live in the region of Hamana not far from Tassey Condé's home village. When the bard was asked about any enduring consequences of Kolonkan's curse, he said the people of Hamana have never done what was needed to lift the curse. He explained that every village in Hamana would need to sacrifice a cow. The tenderloin and internal organs of the cows must be given to the Keita women of Hamana to compensate for the meat that Manden Bori took back from Kolonkan. Each Keita woman must also receive a cloth wrapper to make up for the one that was stripped from Kolonkan in her struggle with Manden Bori. Tassey explained that if the people of Hamana do not make the sacrifice, the curse will never be removed. When he said that, all the elders of Fadama who were present chimed in together, saying, "The curse will be there!"

In the conflict between Kolonkan and her brother, the portrayal of Manden Bori as brash and impetuous reflects many similar images of him to be found in a wide range of epic variants. If the *jeliw* are strikingly consistent in describing Manden Bori as a hotheaded youth, Tassey Condé adds an additional dimension to this character in another episode of intense family drama featuring the opposition of strong-willed siblings. In Sogolon's last important act before dying, she takes her three sons and her daughter Kolonkan outside of town for a private meeting. She reveals that before Maghan Konfara died, he entrusted to her powerful *dalilu* consisting of three things that he had not wanted to bequeath to his eldest son Dankaran Tuman. Sogolon explains that the things are only effective if all three are in the same person's possession, and she asks her sons to agree that these three things should go to Sunjata, since he is the one who was sent for by the people of Manden. The second eldest son, who is called So'olon' Jamori and whom many *jeliw* fail to mention in their performances, insists that the *dalilu* be divided among the three brothers. Sunjata, confident that he can accomplish his destined goals with the *dalilu* that he already possesses, tells Jamori to choose whatever he desires. However, Manden Bori has a bitter dispute with Jamori, who refuses to agree with their mother's wishes. Manden Bori insists that Sunjata take his share, and Sogolon is so grateful that she takes him aside and presents him with the legacy of her ancestors in Dò ni Kiri, a brass finger ring that is said to be the prototype of one of the protective devices still worn by Mande hunters (p. 91).

Several of the most familiar episodes in the Sunjata epic highlight the Manding peoples' interest in all matters involving kinship patterns and family conflicts. One of the most dramatic of these is Tassey Condé's version of the confrontation between Fakoli and his formidable maternal uncle Sumaworo, which results in the nephew's loss of his wife, Keleya Konkon. This is a favorite tale of the *jeliw*, but they often provide only brief accounts, in which Keleya Konkon outshines several hundred of Sumaworo's wives, so he keeps her in Soso and Fakoli angrily returns to Manden. Some of the abbreviated versions are illogical and confusing, with suggestions of incest owing to the family relationship between uncle and nephew. Tassey Condé offers details not usually heard, and he introduces a logical sequence of events that eliminate the apparent confusion found in many versions. According to Tassey's narrative, the fact that Fakoli's natural mother Kosiya Kanté is the sister of Sumaworo, is the source of a vexing dilemma that confronts the hero as Manden and Soso prepare for war. Fakoli explains to the elders of Manden that he cannot join them in their attack on Soso, because that is his mother's homeland. Sunjata concurs, saying he would feel the same way if Manden were to attack his mother's homeland of Dò ni Kiri (p. 95).

Arriving in Soso, Fakoli joins the forces of his uncle Sumaworo, and his wife Keleya Konkon works her magic to outshine Sumaworo's wives in preparing the sacrificial feast for war. The conflict between nephew and uncle arises not from their wives' competition, but from a misunderstanding purposely contrived by conspirators who are threatened by Fakoli's superior abilities and implicit claim to authority as Sumaworo's nephew. Convinced that his nephew has purposely ignored orders to attend a meeting, Sumaworo interprets this and Keleya Konkon's exploits as indications that Fakoli has ambitions to take power in Soso. Sumaworo reminds Fakoli that Keleya Konkon is his own cousin, and that he had received her from Sumaworo in the first place. When he takes Keleya away from Fakoli, the implication is that the woman is returned to her original family to punish and humiliate the nephew for his alleged disloyalty (p. 109). This dramatic falling out within the ruling family of Soso contains the ingredients of classic tragedy and entertains Manding audiences with the delicious irony that the misunderstanding is a major factor in the eventual downfall of Soso, the triumph of Manden, and the founding of the Mali Empire.

Regardless of what ancestral deeds are described in individual episodes of the Sunjata epic, the narratives as recounted by the most erudite bards of Manden are sure to revolve around two principal themes: the complexity of relations between people, and those people's relations with the spirit world. Where human relations are concerned, the oral discourse addresses multiple levels of society as perceived in its most idealized traditional form. Within immediate families, the drama plays out according to partnerships and rivalries between individual wives and their husbands, between competitive co-wives, and between siblings of both genders. The wider village scene employs specifically named archetypal characters representing key occupational groups, including the bards, warriors, hunters, blacksmiths, slaves, merchants, river boatmen, Muslims, and specialists in the occult arts of divination and sorcery. Relations between extended families or clans (*kabilaw*) throughout the lands of Manden feature intricately woven kinship patterns established through politically significant marriages. On the national stage of kingship (*mansaya*) and statehood, charismatic leaders of both genders establish frameworks of power and authority through political intrigue, negotiation with the spirit world, and on occasion, forceful and potentially lethal action.

The outcome of events involving human activity at all levels is at least partly determined by the success or failure of strategies for negotiation with the spirit world, because in the Manding cosmos, everything has a sacred dimension. Diviners draw on whatever sources of occult knowledge or skill are available to them, to identify the sources of their clients' problems and prescribe appropriate sacrifices and other courses of action to reach desired solutions. The most prominent male and female ancestors are masters of magic and medicine who apply their secret knowledge to protect themselves and their people, and to cope with both human and supernatural enemies. As immortal cultural icons, these archetypal heroes and heroines negotiate with genies, render themselves invisible, appear in several places at the same time, and transform themselves into various kinds of living creatures. Such were the tools of the larger-than-life people of legend, who shaped the souls of their descendants and established the kind of history that is valued by traditional Manding societies.

NOTE ON THE MAP OF THE MANDE HEARTLAND (MAP A)

The handmade map labeled "The Mande Heartland and Related *Jamanaw* According to Oral Tradition" is a work in progress that has gradually evolved from an inadequate and erroneous first effort (Conrad 1994: 356) through the more ambitious one included in *Epic Ancestors of the Sunjata Era* (Conrad 1999b: xvii). This map indicates the locations of pre-imperial chiefdoms (*jamanaw*) of the Mande heartland and their neighbors, according to the traditional bards who describe the legendary locations and travels of people active during the life and times of Sunjata.

Previous editions of this map misrepresented the sites of Dakajalan and Kirina. They have traded places and are now in their correct locations. The present edition also includes, the location of the home of Sunjata's father, Maghan Konfara, according to the reservoir of traditional knowledge represented here by Tassey Condé. Tassey refers to the "land of Konfara" and speaks of the people being "in Farakoro" (or Farako); so, pending further clarification, on the map Farakoro is identified as the town, and Konfara as the *jamana*, or chiefdom.[1] Tassey specifies that Konfara was in a swampy region near the present-day town of Kourémalé, which is on the border between Guinea and Mali (l. 75–80), and that it extended up to the location now occupied by the town of Narena in Mali. The alleged location of Farakoro indicates that, according to the extremely knowledgeable bards of Fadama, Sunjata's birthplace was near the Kokoro River, not the Sankarani, which is the popular perception. However, the Sankarani's importance is not diminished in the perception

---

1. Djibril Tamsir Niane, a leading exponent of Niani as the "capital" of the Mali Empire, transcribed the Mansa of Konfara's name as "Maghan Kon Fatta" (1965: 4).

of the Condé bards of Fadama. They believe that when Sunjata returned from exile, he crossed the Sankarani where Niani is located, and that councils were later held in that vicinity.[2] The bard also says that once the issues with Soso were settled, Sunjata founded Maninkoura (New Mani), which is farther north, near where the Sankarani meets the Niger.

State boundaries that were imposed on Africa during the 19th-century European imperial "scramble" for territory have nothing to do with people and events of the Sunjata era, and are not shown on this map. The largest portion of Mande territory represented here is in present-day Mali. Ivory Coast is at the bottom on the right half of the map, on a jagged line running east of Kankan beyond the Wasulu Balé River (not indicated on Map B, "West Africa and Area of Detail"). A section of the Sankarani River running northeast of Niani (Guinea) marks the border between Guinea and Mali for roughly 60 km. In Mali, the Bakoy River passes to the west of Kita before descending to the area of Niagassola in Guinea.

The prominence of rivers as presented on this map reflects the importance they would have always had for economic, strategic, and spiritual reasons. The rivers are located according to their modern-day positions, though in some cases their courses are probably no longer entirely true to what they were in the days of Sogolon and Sunjata. Moreover, the names of some rivers were changed at some time in the past. For example, the Mafou River, which lies southwest of Kouroussa just outside the lower left border of Map A, was, according to Tassey Condé, formerly known as the Balen. Some towns and regional locations that did not exist in the Wagadu or Sunjata eras are included as useful points of reference on the basis of their importance to Manding traditional history in general. Kaarta, Massina, and Baté, for example, all belonged to later centuries, though Tassey Condé does mention them in the comprehensive version of his narrative. For orientation, some familiar modern towns and cities (e.g., Segu, Bamako,

---

2. For discussion on the question of Niani as the town of Sunjata's childhood and the imperial capital, see Conrad 1994.

Sikasso, Siguiri, Kankan) are included in brackets. Identifiable regions from the Sunjata era, such as Wagadu (ancient Ghana), Soso (Sumaworo's kingdom), and Buré (the location of goldfields then and now), are marked in their known locations.

There has been some uncertainty about the location of Sunjata's place of exile with his host Faran Tunkara, because it has been named as both Nema and Mema by various bards. Nema is south of Walata in modern-day Mauritania and within the bounds of Wagadu's ancient location, while Mema is in Mali between Lake Debo and Nampala. Both places are north of old Manden in the sahel, so from the *jeliw* perspective they serve equally well as Sunjata's place of exile. One authoritative source acknowledges both places as part of the larger domain of the Tunkara ruling lineage,[3] which, along with the semantic similarity of the names, helps to account for this duality. Both Mema and Nema are on the map in their known sahelian locations, and Kuntunya is indicated as in the region of Nema because that is where our bard Tassey Condé places it.

The location of one of the most prominent places in the epic, the Kamara *jamana* of Tabon and Sibi, is as well known now as it was in the time of Sunjata, unmistakable owing to the great natural stone arch that towers above some of its villages. Other famous locations, such as the meeting ground of Kurukanfuwa, the battleground at Dakajalan (in some versions identified with nearby Kirina), Dò ni Kiri (the Condé/Diarra *jamana* said to have been in the general region of modern-day Segu), and Negeboriya ("place from which the iron flows"), the *jamana* of Mansa Yèrèlènko, are in approximate locations according to what can presently be understood from oral tradition.

Our narrator Tassey Condé claims the kingdom of Soso consisted of four *jamanaw* ruled by Sumaworo, the names of which are among the Soso ruler's standard praises: Kukuba,

---

3. Youssouf Tata Cissé and Wâ Kamissoko, *Soundjata la gloire du Mali: La grande geste du Mali.* Vol. 2 (Paris, 1991): 37.

Bantamba, Nyemi-Nyemi, and Kambasiga. Some references to these four places tend to be ambiguous. In parts of his narrative, Tassey Condé specifically refers to them as *jamanaw*, but at other times they seem to be towns, and it may be that they are recalled as both in the way that Tabon and Sibi together signify the ancient Kamara *jamana*, though they are individual towns as well (in different locations than they are now, according to local informants). Kukuba, Bantamba, and Nyemi-Nyemi are placed on the map where Maninka *jeliw* of Guinea believe they were located when Sumaworo ruled Soso. The bards believe Kukuba included a powerful stronghold located where Koulouba is now, on the strategic high ground above Bamako, overlooking the Niger. They equate Bantamba with Banamba in the Beledougou region, and claim it was the home of Sumaworo's oracle. At the present stage of research, references to Nyemi-Nyemi seem to point to Niamina, located within the perceived Soso boundaries southeast of the alleged location of Bantamba, on the Niger River. The double utterance in the praising could derive from the fact that one of several Mande villages called "Niani" was near Niamina,[4] with the praise originating as something like "Niani-Niami." Based on textual evidence, the four Soso provinces appear on the map in their rough, general areas pending further research, with question marks to indicate the uncertainty about exact locations.

---

4. Cissé and Kamissoko 1991: 12.

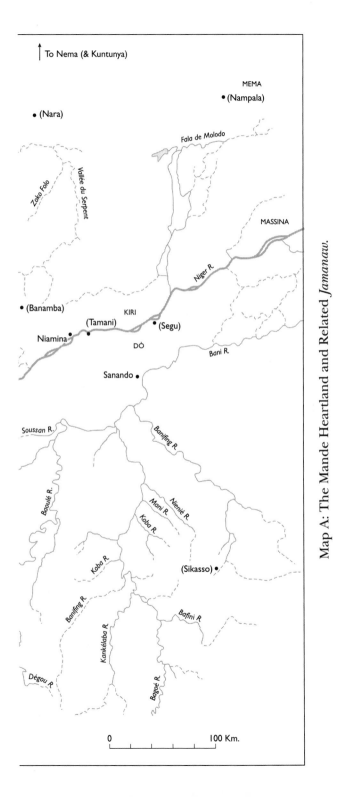

Map A: The Mande Heartland and Related *Jamanaw*.

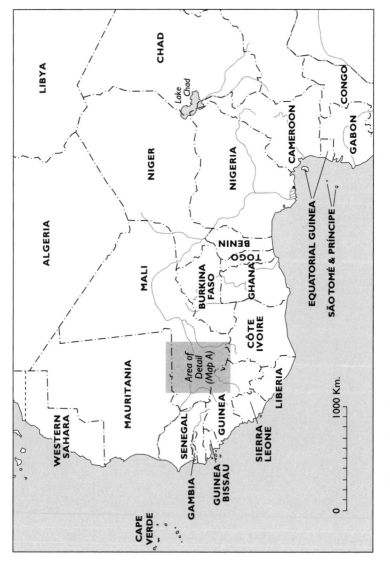

Map B: West Africa and Area of Detail According to Oral Tradition.

SUNJATA

This translation is based on a live oral performance of the Sunjata *epic. Thus the bard addresses his narrative—and his asides and comments—directly to his audience. Readers would do well to picture themselves enjoying the performance seated among an intimate audience on the floor of a small circular thatch-roofed house in sub-Saharan West Africa. (See Introduction, p. xv.)*

BLESSINGS, INTRODUCTIONS, AND PROPHETS OF ISLAM

Allah ho ma salli Allah Muhammadu,
Walali Muhammadi salala Alehu salaamu.[1]

We spent the night in peace. May God give us a peaceful day and save us from hatred and Satan. May God also fulfill the hope with which Dauda Condé, our brother, has come to meet his ancestor and the others gathered to greet him.[2]

All of us—the black-skins and the white-skins—are descended from ancestor Adama. Hawa is our mother;[3] our grandfather is Kémo Poré's son N'fa Namanjan. Though he says I should tell this story, I don't really know enough to tell it as well as he can. He's the master bard, so he should be performing this narrative. Anyone who boasts that they know this story should understand that no matter how well you tell it, there is always someone else who knows it better than you because we all come from Manden.

My name is Tassey Condé, and I have been chosen to tell this story. Djanka Tassey Condé[4]—the younger brother

---

1. Some Maninka bards (*jeliw*) begin their narratives with a Muslim blessing in local, nonstandard Arabic. The phrases invoke the names of God and the Prophet Muhammad, and partially derive from a common phrase used by pious Muslims whenever they mention the Prophet: *ṣallā'llāhu 'alayhi wa-sallama,* "may God bless him and grant him peace."
2. Referring to the visiting researcher—David Conrad—by his Maninka name.
3. Adama and Hawa (Ar. Ḥawwā') = Adam and Eve.
4. In keeping with local custom, Tassey is identified by the name of his mother, Djanka.

of Laye Mamadi Condé,[5] who recently passed away—and I are Fadama Babu's sons.[6] When our father was alive, people came to Fadama for the same reasons you have. May your hopes be fulfilled.

To tell the entire story you've asked about—to start at the very beginning and tell it all the way through—well, that would take all day. In the beginning, God made white-skinned men and black-skinned men. He made three hundred and thirteen prophets[7] and one hundred and twenty-four messengers.[8] All of the one hundred and twenty-four messengers were white men; none of them were black. That's right, all of the messengers were whites, for the black world was not well known in those days. God made blackness after he made whiteness.

The first of the black-skinned men was Sedina Bilali.[9] (The Sunjata you're asking about was a descendant of this Bilali.) If you want to really get into it, all of us—the blacks and whites—were the same people until we were separated into several

5. "Laye" = Al-Hajj ("the pilgrim"). This is either a given name, or signifies that Mamadi had made the pilgrimage to Mecca.

6. Babu Condé of Fadama (d. 1964), one of the best-known and most respected *jeliw* of his time.

7. "Prophets": *alamusanda*. Though Tassey exaggerates the numbers for emphasis, this and the next line accurately reflect the Islamic division of the Prophets into two classes according to their missions. The first category is *Rasūl* (lit. "Messenger," "Envoy"), including Adam, Seth, Noah, Abraham, Ishmael, Moses, Lot, Ṣāliḥ, Hūd, Shu'ayb, Jesus, and Muhammad. These are also referred to in the Koran as *al-mursalun* ("those who are sent"), which is probably the source of Tassey's Maninka term *alamusanda*. In the above list, four prophets were sent specifically to the Arabs: Ṣāliḥ, Hūd, Shu'ayb, and Muhammad.

8. For the second category of Prophets, called *Nabī* (lit. "Prophet," pl. *anbiyā*), The Koran mentions at least twenty-five of them by name, with possible references to at least five additional ones.

9. Bilāl ibn Rabāḥ, a freed black slave of Islamic tradition who became a companion of the Prophet Muhammad and the first caller to prayers. The Mande bards have appropriated him as the Muslim ancestor of Sunjata's Keita lineage.

nations, and then came Paris.[10] We are all Adama's descendants. Our own family's line of descent started with Ibrahima. But we don't need to explain our relationship to you, the Americans, since you and we are both descendants of Isiaaka.[11] You Americans have as much power as any Condé *kamalen.*[12] The only difference is that you have a *dalilu*[13] that we do not have. Just as you have the power in America, we the Condé have the power here in Africa. (That's why we'll brag and get conceited if you start to talk to us about Condé worthiness!) Anyway, we'll not say any more about our common descent from our ancestor Adama since he belongs to all of us.

SEVEN KINGS OF MANDEN

You say you want to know about Manden. We'll have to tell you a lot about Manden; where should we begin? We'll begin with Farako Manko Farakonken of Konfara,[14] who is Ma'an[15] Sunjata's father.

Do you know where Konfara is? It's on the frontier between Guinea and Mali, at a place now called Kourémalé. The swampy area where the Kourémalé people dig their gold mines

---

10. A reference influenced by the French colonial occupation of Guinea, 1898–1958 (see p. xiv).

11. Here Tassey refers to the prophets Abraham and Isaac.

12. Worthy, able young men in their prime (see Glossary).

13. Magic, occult, or secret power; in everyday use, any means used to achieve a goal (see Glossary).

14. The Condé *jeliw* believe Konfara was the *jamana* ruled by Sunjata's father.

15. "Ma'an" is the Maninka contraction of Maghan, an archaic title synonymous with *mansa*, meaning "ruler," or "king."

is known as Konfara, and this place was acquired from us, the Condé. Simbon's[16] father was named after Konfara, even though his real name was Maghan, thus he's known as Maghan Konfara.[17] Maghan Konfara's son was Sunjata, the last *mansa* of Manden.[18] Sunjata was the last of the Mande[19] *mansaw.*

Who was the *mansa* of Manden when Sunjata was born? The first *mansa* of Manden? The very first? That was Donsamogo Diarra, our Condé ancestor. This Donsamogo Diarra was the first son of Ma'an Solonkan, who sired four sons and three daughters. The second of Ma'an Solonkan's sons was Seku Diarra. Then came Mafadu Diarra. The last of Ma'an Solonkan's sons was Kiri Diarra. Those were Ma'an Solonkan's four sons.

Dò Kamissa was the first of Ma'an Solonkan's three daughters. (The killing of Dò Kamissa's buffalo wraith brought Turama'an here; otherwise, the Turama'ans[20] and their ancestors are from Morocco.) The second of Ma'an Solonkan's daughters was Tenenba Condé. (If you hear someone talk about "Soma Tenenba's son Fakoli," well, she raised Fakoli as her own, but she did not give birth to him. A Kanté woman gave birth to Fakoli. They decided to say that Soma Tenenba was Fakoli's mother because she helped him with

---

16. A title of honor carrying the sense of "Master Hunter," used to address any respected leader. The bard applies it to Sunjata, his father, and hunters or warriors at various times in the narrative (e.g., p. 7).

17. The shortened version of the name of Sunjata's father is applied as both name and title.

18. Tassey Condé was aware that there were many kings (*mansaw*) after Sunjata. He means this in the sense of "the greatest of them all." The name "Sunjata" derives from the practice of identifying a male child by his mother's name (cf. n. 4), in this case "Sogolon." Through usage, So'olon Jara (Sogolon's Lion) evolved to various forms, including Son-Jara and Sunjata.

19. When a present-day Maninka bard speaks of "Mande" in the epic, he is referring to Manding peoples living in the heartland of Manden, rather than all Mande language-speaking peoples.

20. Turama'an Traoré's ancestors Abdu Karimi and Abdu Kassimu, later known as Danmansa Wulanni and Danmansa Wulanba.

dalilu.) The third daughter was Sogolon Wulen Condé, and she gave birth to this Sunjata you've asked about.[21]

So Sunjata was born to his father Maghan Konfara, but who were the ancestors of Maghan Konfara? One was Mamadi Kani, who also sired four sons, just as our Condé ancestor did. His sons were: Kani Simbon, Kani Nyogo Simbon, Kabala Simbon, and Big Simbon Madi Tanyagati. Kani Simbon's descendants are the people known as Kulubali. (Kulubali was the first son of Manden. Then came Konaté and Douno. After that came the Mansaré,[22] who are known as Keita.)

Of the seven Mande kings who ruled Manden, the first was Donsamogo Diarra, our Condé ancestor. He fought to gain the Mande kingship. He loved and built Manden. (So those of you who say you are Condé—you have power!)

Next in Manden's leadership was the Kulubali's ancestor, Kani Simbon. Kani Simbon ruled Manden and made it prosperous. He improved Manden without ever going to war; you can't point to anyone who fought against Kulubali. Kulubali ruled and was able to improve Manden without fighting. To the end of his reign, he never fought with anyone.

No battle commander ever captured Kani Simbon, the Kulubali ancestor, just as no war leader ever captured Donsamogo Diarra, the Condé ancestor. From the time my eyes first opened until now, none of our elders has ever said these ancestors were captured in battle by any commander. If you are narrating a history, tell it the way it happened!

---

21. Here and elsewhere (e.g., p. 8), Tassey Condé refers to previous conversations with the researcher.

22. From *mansa*, "king"—i.e., of royal lineage. An honorific for branches of the Keita lineage claiming descent from Sunjata, also applied to patronymics (*jamuw*) related to Sunjata, including the Konaté and Kulubali. Keita: The *jamu* of Sunjata's father was Konaté, but according to tradition, when Sunjata returned from exile to take over the power in Manden, he received the name "Keita."

After Kani Simbon came the Kamara ancestor, Tabon Wana Faran[23] Kamara of Sibi Mountain. That is the Kamanjan[24] you asked about. He did well with Manden and made it prosper. Anyone who rebelled against his rule was captured and brought back into line. He was never captured or defeated in war.

Following Tabon Wana Faran Kamara came Tenen Mansa Konkon of Kirina, the ancestor of the Danaba. He was descended from the Kamissoko. He also did well with Manden. From the beginning to the end of his reign, he was the walking stick that Manden leaned on. (The Kamissoko are in Kirina, and the Kònò of Kirina are their descendants.)

Following Tenen Mansa Konkon was Faran Tunkara of Kuntunya, the Tunkara ancestor. As we'll soon see, Ma'an Sunjata and Manden Bori disappeared into exile in Kuntunya.

The sixth *mansa* was Soso Bali Sumaworo, the Kanté ancestor.

No battle commander ever captured any of the *mansaw* I have just listed. All of these kings made laws and decrees and brought progress to Manden. But they did not unite— that is, the seven regions of Manden did not combine their strength—until it was time for one of them to rule over the whole kingdom; after that, all of the kings supported the one kingdom, right up to the end of his reign.

And when war broke out, it was because of Soso Bali Sumaworo, the sixth *mansa* of Manden

The seventh *mansa* was Ma'an Sunjata. But if we start our story with Ma'an Sunjata—if we do not tell you some of the things that happened before he was born—then we will have left out half the history of Manden. At the time our story begins, Maghan Konfara, Sunjata's father, was *mansa* of the country.

---

23. A title, probably of Soninke origin, that was roughly the equivalent of "Mansa." In Mande epic, it is usually applied to the Kamara ruler of Sibi and Tabon, and to the ruler of Nema/Mema, Faran Tunkara (see p. 74).

24. A nickname, "Tall Kamara," alternative to the ruler's formal title and praise name, Tabon Wana Faran Kamara.

After the reigns of all those other people, God chose Sunjata from among the people; it was God who gave him the power. This is about how Sunjata was born.

THE SEARCH FOR A SPECIAL WIFE

When Maghan Konfara was a *mansa* in Manden, he had power, he had wealth, he was popular, and he had *dalilu*—but he had no child. Maghan Konfara, Sunjata's father, craved a child. Though his friends had begun to have children, he still had no child. But then his *dalilu* showed that he would finally have a child. His *moriw*,[25] his sand diviners, and his pebble diviners[26] all said, "Simbon, you will sire a child who will be famous." Everybody he consulted said the same thing. "But try to marry a light-skinned woman," they told him. "If you marry a light-skinned woman, she will give birth to the child that has been foreseen." Because Maghan Konfara was powerful, he married nine light-skinned women. But aside from Flaba Naabi, none of them gave him a child. He was perplexed. From the last Wednesday of the month of Jomènè[27] to the same time the following year, Maghan Konfara did not sire a child. (If you want to know about Sunjata, then you have to

---

25. Nominal Muslims who, in oral tradition, often perform divination (see Glossary).

26. Seers and healers who identify the source of all kinds of problems by spreading a pile of sand and reading symbols in it, or casting multiple objects such as pebbles or cowrie shells and reading the configurations in which they land. Diviners then prescribe appropriate sacrifices to remedy the problem.

27. The first month of the year.

learn what Sunjata's father and the people of Manden had to endure!)

He sent the *moriw* back into retreat, telling them, "I need a child, so do your best. It's said that if I sire the child that has been foreseen, that child will rule Manden. I must sire this child." The *moriw*, all of whom were present, went back into retreat. When they returned, they told him, "Simbon, marry somebody who is a mulatto." So he married nine mulatto women. But aside from Marabajan Tarawelé, none of those mulatto women gave birth. From that time of the year to the same time the following year, none of those women who were with him in the house bore any male children. Simbon was frustrated. Maghan Konfara sent the *moriw* back into retreat. He said, "Tell me the truth. Ah! If you see that I will not have any children, tell me. A child is something that only God can provide; it cannot be bought in the market." This time the *moriw* told him, "very well, marry a black woman. Find a black woman who has a white heart." This time he married nine black women. But aside from Nyuma Damba Magasuba, none of them bore any children.

Maghan Konfara was frustrated. His *moriw* told him again, "very well, man, free one of your slave girls and marry her." (In those days they still practiced slavery.) He liberated and married nine slave girls. But aside from Jonmusoni Manyan, none of the slave girls bore him any children. Frustrated, Simbon gathered the people of Konfara together on the last Wednesday of Jomènè.

When the people of Konfara had gathered, he separated the *moriw*, the sand diviners, and the pebble diviners into groups and sent them all into retreat. He said, "I told you not to hesitate. If you see that I won't have a child, tell me. Go into the house. If you do not tell me the truth, I'll kill all of you and replace you." When the *moriw* came out of retreat, they told him, "Simbon, you will sire a child. Make one of your *jelimusow*[28] happy. Marry her so she will give birth." He

---

28. Female bards (sing. *jelimuso*).

made nine *jelimusow* happy, but aside from Tunku Manyan Diawara, none of them ever gave birth.

Now all of Manden was frustrated. (It's hard to give birth to a child who will be famous!) And when all of Manden became frustrated, the diviners were ashamed of themselves. They met and swore an oath: "Any one of us who has broken a taboo should confess it. Maybe this is our fault. If we don't get together and tell this man the truth, the feet of our descendants will not be able to even break an egg in Manden." They went into retreat and came back out, telling Simbon, "Someone will come from the East. He will be coming from the land of the white-skinned people. This much has been revealed to us. Let this man pray to God for a solution to your problem. If you let this man pray to God on the matter of your son, anything he tells you will be God's word. We won't be able to accomplish this ourselves. God has shown us a good man."

While they waited there in Farakoro,[29] Manjan Bereté arrived. Manjan Bereté was the first Muslim leader of Manden; he opened the door[30] to the Mande people. (He is also the ancestor of the Bereté in Manden. The home of the Bereté people is Farisini Hejaji,[31] a region in the land of Mecca; the Bereté are Suraka.[32]) Bereté packed up some books and came from Farisi to the land of Manden because it was a powerful place. If he found someone in the land of Manden who would join him, who would work with the Koran, then his blessings would be great. Because he could

29. Sometimes shortened to "Farako." Evidently the hometown of Sunjata's father, located in the territory (*jamana*) of Konfara. Farakoro appears in the longer version of Maghan Konfara's name, as he was known to Tassey Condé and his ancestral bards of Fadama: Farako Manko Farakonken.

30. That is, he was instrumental in the introduction of Islam.

31. "Farisi" is from Fars, a region in Persia. "Hejaji" is from Hejaz, a region that was the ancient cradle of Islam, including the Red Sea coast of Arabia and the cities of Mecca, Medina, and others.

32. A Maninka and Bamana term for the local perception of "Arab," which includes "Moors" and North Africans in general.

not get used to the food here, Manjan Bereté brought Sansun Bereté, his little sister, with him when he came to meet
Simbon. He brought his sister so she could prepare his food
until he became better acquainted with the Mande people.

Manjan Bereté came and lived with Simbon. He said, "You
need the religion practiced in my homeland. The Prophet
has said nobody should take up swords in the religion again,
that we should now be gentle with one another. Let us win
people over with kindness, so we can awaken their minds and
they can join the religion. The blessings will be great for anyone who accomplishes this."

Simbon welcomed Manjan Bereté and his sister when they
came to live with him. After Simbon welcomed them, his wife
Jonmusoni Manyan went to him and said, "Simbon, aah, it
seems to me that this is the man described by your diviners.
Because every day since he arrived he has washed his feet and
prayed at two o'clock. And every day at four o'clock he has
washed his feet and prayed. And at seven o'clock he washes
his feet and prays. When it is eight o'clock I can still hear him
praying in his room. Get closer to this man. How can you just
sit here? Do not allow every stranger to flow past you like a
river; a citizen's well-being arrives in the form of a stranger."

So Maghan Konfara went to Karamogo[33] Bereté. He
observed that the *karamogo* was so clean that fresh milk could
be seen flowing down his throat when he drank it. Maghan
Konfara said to him, "Karamogo, forgive me. It has been a
long time since you arrived, but I have now come to greet you.
You came and found me troubled. Come here and I will show
you the cause of my worry." Taking the teacher by the hand,
Maghan Konfara opened his gate and showed him all his barren wives. He said, "You see all of these women? Among them
are light-skinned women, black-skinned women, bards, and
slaves. Your arrival was foretold before you came; pray to God
for me, so that I can sire a son."

---

33. "Teacher." As the proper noun "Karamogo," an honorific for a distinguished Muslim community leader, signifying a respected scholar,
learned one, wise man.

Bereté had come so that his kind[34] would be better known. He was devoted to his faith, and he had never violated a taboo. Maghan Konfara was pleased to have him in Manden. Bereté went into retreat and prayed to God, and God replied, saying Maghan Konfara should marry a woman with the same totem as the Bereté. God told Bereté that if Maghan Konfara married a woman with the same totem as the *karamogo*, he would sire a child. Oh! And what was his totem? God said, "You came and saw them and they were not praying." So Bereté told Maghan Konfara, "You must marry the daughter of someone who prays."

Once Simbon heard this, he said "Ha! Karamogo, I am very fortunate. Though I promised to pray, I have been so occupied with my chiefly duties that I have not kept that promise. Though you have prayed every day at prayer time, you have not seen me praying. Perhaps my totem wife[35] is among those now within the yard. Maybe we are related through marriage.[36] Since you have come, you are my totem. Please give me the little sister who accompanied you here."

The Karamogo said, "I can't do that."

"Why not?"

"We can't go from white to black. We are Bereté. It was our ancestor who planted the Prophet's date farm at Mecca; that was the beginning of our family's identity. When we planted the date farm for the Prophet, he blessed our ancestor. He said everyone should leave us alone: *Bè anu to yè*, and that is why they call us Bereté.[37] No man here will tell you that we made up the Bereté family identity. It was the

---

34. Muslims.

35. A woman with the same totem as the Bereté. The "totem" (Maninka *tana*, Bamana *t'né, tènè*) is a sacred animal or plant that, according to legend, saved the life of an ancestor of a particular family, and thus must never be killed or eaten by a member of that family. Elsewhere in this narrative, *tana* is translated as "taboo," where it refers to a sacred object that must not be touched or used by anyone but the owner.

36. Suggesting they might be cousins.

37. Such explanations for the origins of names of people and places are based on folklore and are called popular etymologies.

Prophet who said we should be set apart, that nobody's fool-
ishness should trouble us. *Bè anu to yè,* everyone should leave
us alone. Thus we became the Bereté. From that time up to
today, we have not done anything other than the Prophet's
business.

"This place has already become impious because of your
lack of attention to Islam. So how can I give you my little sister? I did not come from Farisi for that purpose, so I will not
give you my little sister."

"Aaah," said Simbon, "give her to me. If you want wealth,
I'll give you wealth. But if you do not give her to me, I'll take
her for myself anyway, because you are not in your home, you
are in my home."

When Manjan Bereté was told this, he said, "If you take
my sister for yourself, I'll go back to Farisi. I'll go and get
Suraka warriors to destroy Manden if you take my little sister
by force."

Simbon said, "You just do that. Maybe if you go back to
Farisi to get warriors, you will come and destroy Manden. But
by then your sister will be pregnant. I'll have a child by then.
Even if I die, it will still be my child. It's already done; I have
taken her." And so he took Manjan Bereté's little sister. "If
you call for wealth, I'll give you wealth. If you call for the
sword, I'll agree to that. I have the power; you have no power,
you are in my place."

Manjan Bereté packed up his books and returned to Farisi.
He went and told his fathers and brothers, "The Mande
mansa I visited has used his chiefly power to take my little
sister from me."

His fathers and brothers said, "Ah, Manjan Bereté, your
youth has betrayed you. You carry the sacred book. You've
been looking for someone to help you with the work of the
sacred book. Go back and tell the Mande people, tell Simbon, that if he is in love with your younger sister, you'll give
him both her and the book. Tell him, 'If you convert and
become another like me, so that we can proselytize together,
I'll give you my younger sister. But if you refuse to convert, I'll
go get my warriors.' If he does not convert, come back and

we'll give you warriors. If he agrees to convert, well, that is what you went for in the first place."

Manjan Bereté returned to Farakoro. After he explained all of this to Simbon, Maghan Konfara said, "Your father is right! Your youth did betray you. If you had done what he said in the first place, you would not have returned to Farisi. All I want is a child, no matter what the cost. So I agree to what you propose. Since you have requested that I convert, I agree."

They shaved his head,[38] and together they read the Koran. After reading the Koran, Manjan Bereté gave his little sister to Maghan Konfara. Manjan Bereté's sister was called Sansun Bereté. Sansun Bereté first gave birth to Maghan Konfara's son called Dankaran Tuman; he was older than Ma'an Sunjata. After bearing that one son, she had a daughter who was called Nana Triban. She only gave birth to that one son and that one daughter.

After siring those two children, Simbon became troubled again. He said, "Karamogo! Go back into retreat. If my son Dankaran Tuman, your nephew, is the son that has been foretold, let me know. But also let me know if this son is not the one that was prophesied. We should not lie to one another."

Manjan Bereté went into retreat. He prayed to God. God revealed to him that Dankaran Tuman was not the son that was foretold. He came out and told Simbon that a trumpet would be blown when the foretold son was born, and that the child's name would never disappear. He said, "Dankaran Tuman is not the son."

Simbon said, "How do I get that son? Pray to God for me to have that son. Will I get that son?"

"Yes, you will get that son."

"Very well, pray to God for that."

Manjan Bereté prayed to God. He said, "Simbon, you will get this child. When I was praying, God revealed to me that there are others like me who will come. They too will come from the land of the white-skins. Those people will not bring

---

38. Signifying that the person had become a Muslim.

any woman with them when they come. But they will tell you the name of the place that is their destination, and if you ask them to, they will bring you a woman from that place. She will bear that child."

[In an omitted passage, the narrator describes the Moroccan background of two brothers, Abdu Karimi and Abdu Kassimu, who will travel to the land of Dò ni Kiri to hunt a buffalo that is devastating the countryside, and will eventually become known as Danmansa Wulanni and Danmansa Wulanba.]

TWO HUNTERS ARRIVE IN MANDEN

Abdu Karimi and Abdu Kassimu came to Manden from Morocco. When they got here they walked all night and all the following day, and were already under the three *nkiliki* trees of Manden by the evening of that second day. When Abdu Karimi and Abdu Kassimu arrived under the trees, they measured out their food, cooked their meal, ate, and slept there.

(People used to rest under those three *nkiliki* trees when traveling to and from Dò ni Kiri, the home of the Condé. Travelers of Manden, from the home of the Mansaré, used to rest there, as did travelers from Negeboriya, the home of the Koroma. Travelers from Soso, from the home of the Kanté, also used to rest under those trees. People could get the news of the world there.)

Abdu Karimi and Abdu Kassimu, who were Arab *kamalenw*, were worried, for they did not know where they were headed.

They found a place where some traders had left their cooking pots. After eating, the Arab *kamalenw* said, "Let's lie down here and wait for these traders to return. We'll soon learn our next destination."

While Abdu Karimi and Abdu Kassimu were sleeping, some traders who were on their way from Manden arrived. Some traders also arrived from Negeboriya, home of the Koroma. They all greeted one another.

The Arab *kamalenw* asked, "Is everything all right with the people of Manden?"

The traders replied, "There is nothing wrong with them."

"Is everything all right with the Koroma of Negeboriya?"

The traders said, "Nothing is troubling them." They too measured out their food; then they went to sleep.

While the brothers were lying there, some traders who were on their way from Soso arrived. These traders had visited Dò ni Kiri and found it in turmoil. Upon meeting Abdu Karimi and Abdu Kassimu, they asked, "Where are you from?"

The *kamalenw* said, "We are from Morocco."

"Where are you going?"

The *kamalenw* replied, "We were on our way to the land of the Condé, but we don't know the way."

The traders said, "The *mansa* of Dò ni Kiri is Donsamogo Diarra; he is quarreling with his sister."

I just told you about this sister, called Dò Kamissa, the first daughter of Ma'an Solonkan. She and her brother, Donsamogo Diarra, were quarreling over the issue of the legacy left by Ma'an Solonkan, their mother.

Dò Kamissa said, "Donsamogo Diarra, if you refuse to share our mother's legacy with me, I'll take it myself."

The Condé elders said to her, "Go ahead and *try* to take a share for yourself; you are too headstrong."

"You think I can't take it for myself?"

"Yes, that's right." They did not know she had the power to transform herself into different things.

Dò Kamissa left the town and stayed in a farm hamlet near Dò ni Kiri. At that time, the place known as Dò ni Kiri included the twelve towns of Dò, the four towns of Kiri, and the six towns on the other side of the river. At the break of day, Dò Kamissa transformed herself into a buffalo and began to kill the people living in those places.

It became a bad time for Dò ni Kiri.

Donsamogo Diarra said, "This buffalo has killed all of the hunters that I requested from Manden." He sent a message to the Koroma of Negeboriya, but the buffalo killed all of the hunters who came from there. He sent for the hunters of Soso, but when they came the buffalo killed them all, too.

Donsamogo Diarra was at a loss. He sent out the word from Dò ni Kiri. He said, "People have died because of me. Anyone who kills this buffalo will get to choose a wife from three age sets[39] of Dò ni Kiri's girls." Everybody who visited Dò ni Kiri was told about this. And when the traders returned to the camp under the *nkiliki* tree, they told Abdu Karimi and Abdu Kassimu about the turmoil in Dò ni Kiri.

The traders said, "Things in Dò ni Kiri have become very bad. Donsamogo Diarra's quarrel with his sister has resulted in many deaths. Hunger has come to Kiri because no one can go in or out. The paths to the village and farms have been closed. There is no way for crops to be brought home, for the buffalo is blocking the way. The Condé say that anyone who kills this buffalo will get to choose a wife from three sets of Dò ni Kiri girls."

The Arab *kamalenw* were still camped there. The younger brother, Abdu Karimi, said, "Big brother, do you hear what they are saying?"

Abdu Kassimu replied, "I hear it."

Together they said, "Let us go to Dò ni Kiri."

The elder brother said, "Hey, little brother, what about these things they are talking about? Suppose the buffalo kills us?"

Abdu Karimi replied, "If the buffalo kills us, at least we'll die for the sake of the Condé. They are having a bad time in

---

39. Children born within the same span of about three years are identified as a single group or age set that grows up together, going through the various initiation rituals into adulthood.

Dò ni Kiri. I feel bad for them. Remember how our fathers
told us the story of the Condé ancestor Samasuna?[40] Before
the Prophet could make any progress, God told him to fight
at Kaïbara.[41] The Condé ancestor Samasuna took a thousand
of his sons to go and help our ancestors fight at the battle of
Kaïbara, and there he lost all thousand of his sons. No matter
how difficult the fight at Dò ni Kiri will be, it can't be more
difficult than the battle at Kaïbara.

"The thousand sons that the Condé ancestor Samasuna
gave all died on the battleground of our ancestors' war at
Kaïbara. If the two of us should die for the sake of the Condé,
will our deaths be equal to the deaths of those thousand men?
If it's our time to die, we should die for a good cause. We do
not equal a thousand men. But if we should die for the sake
of the Condé, we will only be doing what the thousand men
did for those ancestors. So let us go to Dò ni Kiri. Knowing
what the Condé ancestors suffered for our sake at Kaïbara,
we would be bastards if we retreated now, after hearing that
the Condé are suffering." Thus Abdu Karimi encouraged his
elder brother.

Abdu Kassimu now had the courage to go to Dò ni Kiri.
But first the brothers packed their belongings and went
straight to Konfara. They bypassed Dò ni Kiri and went
straight to Manden.

When the brothers arrived in Manden, Manjan Bereté
was sitting in a circle near Maghan Konfara. The two men
were playing *wari*.[42] Manjan Bereté was sitting in the circle
near Simbon, with prayer beads in his hands, praying to God:
"May God not let me be embarrassed by my prediction." They

---

40. Samson (Ar. S̲h̲amsūn) is not mentioned in the Koran, but according to other sources of Muslim tradition (e.g., al-Tha'labi and al-Tabari),
he dedicated his life to God and continually fought against idolators.

41. Maninka usage of Khaybar, an oasis ninety-five miles from Medina,
Arabia, the site of a famous battle fought by the prophet Muhammad
and his army.

42. A popular game played with two rows of shallow holes, usually
in a carved wooden board, with small stones or cowrie shells used as
counters.

remained sitting when they saw Abdu Karimi and Abdu Kassimu approaching. When the two brothers arrived, all of the men met in that same circle, and Manjan Bereté and Maghan Konfara stopped playing *wari*.

Abdu Karimi said, "My respected *karamogo*, we have come to God, we have come to the Mande people, and we have come to Simbon. What makes us walk fast will also make us talk fast."

After greeting the brothers, the Mande people asked them, "Where did you come from?"

The Arab *kamalenw* said, "We come from Morocco."

"What is your family?"

"We are Sharifu."[43]

The Mande people saluted them, "You Haidara,"[44] to which the *kamalenw* replied, "Marahaba."[45]

The Mande people said, "The honor is yours, the honor is Simbon's."

The Arab *kamalenw* said, "We come from Morocco. We are children of Abdu Sharifu. We are descendants of Saïdina Ali."[46]

The *kamalenw* explained, "We have heard that the Condé are suffering, that they are quarreling with their sister who has transformed herself into a buffalo. Every morning the buffalo has killed people in all of the twelve towns of Dò, the four towns of Kiri, and the six towns across the river. That is why we have come. We want to go to Dò ni Kiri, to

---

43. Contraction of the longer plural form Sharifulu (p. 40) from the Arabic Shurafa' (sing. Sharīf), a lineage claiming descent from the family of the Prophet Muhammad.

44. A prestigious Muslim family name in Manden, here used in a greeting as the equivalent of Sharifu.

45. Response to a greeting that honors people by saluting their ancestors with the family name or *jamu* (patronymic, identity). From Ar. *mrehba* ("welcome").

46. ʿAlī ibn Abī Ṭālib, cousin and son-in-law of the Prophet Muhammad, one of the first converts to Islam; renowned as a warrior during Islam's struggle for survival, he took part in most of the Prophet's expeditions and displayed legendary courage at the battles of Badr and Khaybar.

help the Condé with their trouble. We want you to perform
the sand divination for us. If our sand is sweet, we will go to
Dò ni Kiri. And if our sand is not sweet, we will still go to
Dò ni Kiri."

Simbon chuckled. He said, "Ah, my men! Manhood is in
the mouth. If a man does not understand what you are saying, he might attack you. You say that if the sand is sweet you
will go! And if the sand is not sweet you will still go?"

They said, "Uh huh, we will still go."

Simbon said, "Ah, blessings upon you."

After giving the two brothers lodgings in a house, Simbon went into his room and spread the divination sand. He
spread and spread and spread the sand, and said the words
over it. He said, "If these boys are the source I have been told
about, if they go to Dò ni Kiri, will they kill the buffalo? Let
the sand be sweet."

When he spread the sand, he saw that it was sweet for
them. Alone in his room, he spread the sand three times.
When the sand was sweet, he sent for the boys, saying, "Come
here. Come and let me spread the sand in your presence."

When the sand was spread, Abdu Karimi was pleased. Simbon told them, "You, Sharifu, your sand is good. Your sand is
sweet, but there is a sacrifice to be made."

"What sacrifice?"

"A complicated one."

"What is it?"

"Offer three piles of peanuts. Go and pick some old straw
out of a roof, light it on fire, and roast the peanuts. Call the
little children to come. While the children are eating the
peanuts, you should stand nearby with your quiver of arrows.
When the children are finished eating the peanuts, have them
stand up and say, 'May God answer this sacrifice.' You respond
to that with 'Amina.' And by the grace of God, your sand will
be sweet."

Simbon said, "I will offer the peanuts." He made the peanut offering. He set the peanuts out in three piles. He went
to his wives' cookhouse, picked some old thatch out of the
roof, and lit it on fire.

The hunters prepared themselves while the peanuts were roasting. (People of early times did not carry much baggage.) When they were dressed, they went and stood near the little children. Once the children had finished eating the peanuts—just as the children were about to leave—the hunters said, "May God answer this sacrifice."

As the hunters were leaving, Maghan Konfara said, "You Sharifu, the Condé have said that they will offer three groups of girls to whoever kills this buffalo, and that whoever kills the buffalo can choose a wife from these girls. You will kill the buffalo. When they bring the young girls to you, you should pick one as a wife for me." (What if you said that to someone and they did not bring the wife?)

The arrogant younger brother Abdu Karimi said, "I will not answer him; I am looking for a wife for my elder brother." The hunters departed.

[In an omitted passage, the narrator introduces the buffalo's female genie companion, who advises the brothers on how to respond to abusive women they will meet, and how to approach Dò Kamissa, the Buffalo Woman, and avoid being killed by her.]

DÒ KAMISSA THE BUFFALO WOMAN

After walking for one kilometer, the brothers passed into the land of Konfara, and from there crossed into the land of the Condé. There they met a woman who had borne one child, just as the female genie had told them. The genie had said, "You will not see me again. But if you don't heed the advice I give you, the buffalo will kill you."

When they greeted this woman who had borne one child, she spoke abusively to them. She said, "Eh! Is it the woman who should greet first, or is it the man? You do not pass by a beautiful woman without greeting her!" She said every possible bad word to them.

They said, "M'ba. We are children of the road. We do not know anything about women or men. We have never been to this country. We speak to everyone we meet, so they can help us."

She replied, "Am I the one who is supposed to help you?"

Huh! They passed on by her without quarreling further.

After they passed that woman, they walked another kilometer and met the full-breasted girl. When they met this girl they said, "Lady, we greet you, God is great."

Ah! She abused them. She said every bad word to them.

The younger brother said, "Aaah, you do not understand. A beautiful woman like you will pass by a man like that? You do not know what is happening." (No matter how proud a girl is, once you call her "beautiful," she will soften.)

After the hunters passed by the full-breasted girl, she went on her way. (Humility really comes only with death, but men act humbly until they get what they want.)

After walking on for another kilometer, they heard the pounding of the mortars and pestles[47] of Dò ni Kiri, and there they met Dò Kamissa herself. She carried a hoe on her shoulder and a walking staff served as her third leg.

When they said, "Greetings mother." Heeeh! She cursed their father. After that, she cursed their grandfather. Then she cursed their mother.

"You are calling me mother? Was I the one who gave birth to your father or your mother?" She said every bad word to them.

Abdu Karimi said, "Big brother, don't you think this lady resembles our mother?"

---

47. The mortar is a large wooden receptacle in which women pound grain with a heavy, wooden, club-shaped pestle that can be as long as five feet.

Abdu Kassimu replied, "Heeh, this lady does resemble our mother. Everything she is doing to us seems familiar."

Abdu Karimi said, "This lady abuses us the same way our own mother abuses us. Hey! Look at the way she walks, just like our mother."

Abdu Kassimu said, "Ma, where are you going?"

She said, "Do I have to explain anything to you? I am going to look for termites to feed my chickens."

Abdu Karimi said, "Ah, big brother, hold my bag." He reached out to take the hoe from the old woman. He said, "Give me your hoe; I will dig termites for your chickens."

She replied, "When I look for termites, are you the one who always feeds my chickens? If you don't let go of my hoe, you'll soon get what's coming to you."

They scuffled over the hoe until Abdu Karimi took it from the old lady. When he got the hoe from her he dug for termites, put them in a bag, and loaded them on his head.

The older brother, Abdu Kassimu, had Abdu Karimi's baggage. He said, "Let's go."

When they got some distance ahead of the woman, Abdu Karimi said, "Big brother, let's be careful, because this woman is the buffalo the female genie told us about. You see the way this old woman looks? Let's watch her carefully and walk briskly. If we leave her behind, it will mean that the person we are looking for is still ahead of us. But if we can't leave her behind, then we'll know that she is the buffalo we were told about."

The two men walked very briskly. The old woman was behind them. As they walked—*chu, chu, chu!*—they looked back and saw the old woman was still behind them.

The younger brother said, "Didn't I tell you she is the one?"

When they reached the path to Dò ni Kiri, the way leading to the old woman's hamlet branched off to the right. The way to Dò ni Kiri branched off to the left. When the brothers started to take the big path to Dò ni Kiri, the old woman said, "Where are you going with my termites?" Then they knew she was the buffalo for sure.

She said, "Don't you know what happened between me and the men of Dò ni Kiri? So why did you take my hoe from

me? If the termites belong to me, why are you taking that
path? Don't you see my path?"

The hunters took the path to Dò ni Kiri.

*[In omitted passages, the narrator names various groups of genies
that support the Buffalo Woman, describes the Kulubali regime
when Dò ni Kiri became known as Bambarana, and explains
how Maninka warriors distinguished between themselves and the
enemy in early times.]*

When the hunters arrived in Dò ni Kiri, God caused Ma
Sogolon's sister Dò Kamissa to soften toward them. Every
other person, every hunter who had come to kill the buffalo,
was dead.

A bird that lived near Dò Kamissa's swamp was the buffalo
woman's spy. If someone entered her swamp, the bird would
call, *tumè-tumè*—and as soon as the bird did that, the buffalo
woman would go out and kill them. That bird is still acting as
her spy today! If you go into the swamp in the middle of the
night, you will hear it calling out, "Someone is here!"

Many wild creatures were on the buffalo woman's side. She
had a wild cat. That wild cat and the tree squirrel would steal
the Condé's chickens for her. The leopard and the hyena
would steal the Condé's cattle. The animals attacked all of
our[48] livestock.

The quarrel had now reached a critical stage. Dò Kamissa
and her genies were also attacking the people of Dò ni Kiri. By
now, this buffalo woman had made widows of many women,
caused many men to lose their wives, and taken many children from their parents.

The Arab *kamalenw* arrived in Dò ni Kiri just as all of this
was going on. After they greeted our ancestor Donsamogo
Diarra, he asked them, "How did you get here?"

They said, "Thanks to God."

---

48. The Condé of Fadama trace their lineage directly back to the
ancient Condé/Diarra family of Dò ni Kiri.

"Ah!" he said. "Where did you come from?"

"We come from Morocco."

"What is your family name?"

"We are Sharifu."

Donsamogo Diarra saluted them, "You Haidara," to which they replied, "Marahaba."

Donsamogo Diarra asked, "Why have you come here? Haven't you heard about the trouble here? Haven't you heard that my sister Dò Kamissa has killed my people? Should it be said that Sharifu wasted their blood in the land of the Condé?[49] Huh? You Sharifu, I'm not pleased with you coming here. I'm not pleased to see you."

They said, "Allah!"

"Very well, if it is God who has sent you, don't go into the bush. Stay in town and I will assemble my children. I'll give them to you so you can teach them. Just don't go into the bush. I don't want this country cursed because a Sharif dies on my land. Dò ni Kiri must not be cursed."

The Arab *kamalenw* said, "Very well," and were given lodgings in a house. The buffalo woman was somewhere else, thank God.

A day or two after the *kamalenw* had settled into a house, their hosts killed a chicken for them. When the chicken was killed, the brothers put the sauce on the rice, took a chicken thigh and backbone, and put them into the saucepan. Then they went out the back door and took the food to the bad old buffalo woman in the bush. When they got there they said, "Ma, didn't we both tell you that you resemble our mother? For God's sake, we can't deny it; you do resemble our mother. Heh, we didn't even want to leave you when we did. We came to town and your brother killed a chicken for us. In Morocco, when we kill a chicken, we give our mother the backbone. We give our father the thigh. You are our mother and our

---

49. As descendants of the Prophet Muhammad (see n. 43), they are Muslim elite, so he wants them to stay out of danger and give his children Koranic lessons.

father—so what goes to our father, what goes to our mother, is all yours."

She reached out her hand, took the food and the sauce, and threw it at them. She said, "Why did you bring the termites? When you brought the termites, was it not for the chickens? When you left, did I tell you I had a craving for chicken meat? Sharifu, stop trying to get what you want from me. You're being stubborn. If it weren't for the relationship between the Sharifu and the Condé, I'd kill you just like all the others for what you are doing to me now. Won't you leave me alone? I am talking to you."

The *kamalenw* took the sauce and returned to town.

After one or two days, another chicken was killed for the brothers. They did the same thing as before and took the pieces to the bad old buffalo woman in the bush. She took the food and gave it to the dogs, repeating the same words she'd said before. The brothers returned to town.

After another one or two days, the Condé killed another chicken. The *kamalenw* visited the old woman again. This time, when they came to her, she took the chicken pieces and put them on the shelf. Then she spoke to them the words that were in her mouth: "I know you're strangers. Haven't you talked to some local people?"

"Ah!" said the brothers. "Old woman, we have talked to some natives."

She herself was reluctant to tell them that she had killed local people. But if they had talked to some local people, they would have heard about the mayhem she'd caused. The *kamalenw* did not let on that they knew.

They just said, "Old woman, we have spoken with some local people."

"Ah! Didn't they tell you anything?"

"Ah! They told us that an old woman, their sister, has gone away, and that they seek blessings from this sister who is out of town. They did not tell us anything else. We come from Morocco; we don't know anything. We are looking for blessings from our mothers. Do whatever you want to us." Then they went on their way.

If the hunters had said to her, "Your brothers say that you
have caused them suffering, that you have killed off their
people," she would have thought that they were reproach-
ing her. So they did not say that. (That is why when you go
visiting, you should not tell your hosts what is going on back
home. If you report on what is being discussed at home, you
will not be able to accomplish your mission.)

The next time a chicken was killed, the Arab *kamalenw*
took the road back to the old lady. When they met her, they
said, "Ma, didn't we tell you? We will not eat our mother's or
father's share as long as you are here, until we finish with our
visit and return home. Nobody in town will eat your share. So
to whom should we give this food?"

When she took it from them, they started to leave. But
then she said "Sharifu, take your seats."

They sat down.

DÒ KAMISSA'S REVELATIONS

Dò Kamissa the Buffalo Woman said, "You have outdone
me. No one can get the better of people like you. You are
polite. You were brought up well. Eh! Despite everything you
were told, you were not discouraged. You favor me? Now I
will cooperate with you. Were it not for you, I would have
wiped out Dò ni Kiri.

"You know that Donsamogo Diarra, with whom I am quarreling, is my brother. I was the firstborn of my father's children. When I reached puberty, I said, 'My Lord God, I will
give the largest of the two gold earrings that are on my ears
to whoever brings me the news that my father has had a son.
My Lord God, I will also give the beautiful outer one of the
two wrappers I am wearing to the person that brings me such

good news.' I was the first to offer a sacrifice for my brother. So who does he think he is, telling me that women shouldn't have property? Huh!

"I would have wiped out Donsamogo's entire lineage. But you Sharifu, you have outdone me. I will cooperate with you and give you my life, for I know that if you kill me, you will bury me; you will not let my body go to God as a bad body.

"Before I give myself up to you, though, I will ask you to do three things for me. If you agree to do those three things, then I will cooperate with you. But if you do not agree to those three things, I will keep after you until you do."

The *kamalenw* said, "Ma, tell us the three things you want us to do for you."

She said, "Here's the first: Don't go to town immediately after killing the buffalo; come to this hamlet instead. You'll find me dead. Because I am the only one who knows what I have done,[50] my brother must not see my corpse. When you arrive here, you'll see that I have poured water on the fire. There will be a hoe; there will also be an axe. Take the axe and cut down a *toro* tree. Take the hoe and dig my grave. After you have laid me in it, fire the musket. At no point can my brother, my father's son, see my body; nor can my body be carried to Dò ni Kiri. I have not done any good for them. I have wiped out their children, I have wiped out their wives, I have widowed their husbands; this is all my doing.

"That's the first thing you must do. Now, you know that whoever kills me will be rewarded with the choice of a wife from three sets of Dò ni Kiri's girls. The second thing you must do for me is refuse all of the fine young girls they bring out for you. Do not choose any of those girls as your wife, because they would be forcing my father's last-born to remain in the house. Five sets of girls have gone to their husbands, but she has not married, and if you do not marry her, she will never be married. She holds something special in her breast for whoever marries her. You, Sharifu, must marry her.

---

50. Contrary to what the narrator has previously indicated.

"She is very ugly. She's the 'Short Sogolon' you've heard about, the one who is so very ugly. I damaged one of her tear ducts and now her eyes water all the time. Her head is bald, she has a humped back, her feet are twisted, and when she walks, she limps this way and that. I, Dò Kamissa, did all of that to her.

"How could I make her so ugly when I loved her so much? I put my far-seeing mask[51] on her face before she was old enough to wear it, and, in doing so, cut her tear duct, caused her hair to fall out, and put a hump on her back. By putting her on my sorcery horse when she was too young, I twisted her feet, stretched her tendons, and made her knock-kneed. All of this is my fault. I take the blame, and if she does not get married, it will be my curse.

"So, when the men of Dò ni Kiri bring those beautiful Condé women to you, do not accept any of them. Choose my father's last-born. Some call her 'Humpbacked Sogolon.' Some call her 'Ugly Sogolon.' Everybody used to call her whatever they felt like. But the real name of that last-born child is Sogolon Wulen Condé. There will be something special in her breast for you because she'll have all the *dalilu*.[52]

"If you choose her over all the beautiful daughters they offer you and are not satisfied with the way she looks, then cut off the buffalo's tail when you kill it. The tail is heavy with gold and silver, because I took the gold and silver earrings of every Dò ni Kiri woman I killed and hung them from the hair of my tail. I have a lot of hair on my tail, and it is heavy with the gold and silver ear jewelry of the Dò ni Kiri women. If you exchange some of that gold, you can go and marry a beautiful woman somewhere else, a wife to have along with Sogolon Condé. But do not refuse to take

---

51. A magic object allowing the wearer to see unimaginable distances. The concept might have entered oral tradition when Europeans were observed using telescopes and binoculars, but there also could have been an indigenous mask imbued with such power.

52. The mother's physical deformities signal her possession of special occult powers that she will pass on to her child.

Sogolon! Then there will be no problems. Will you do this, or not?"

The Sharifu said, "We agree to that."

She said, "That is the second thing you must do. Here's the third thing: the dead buffalo's carcass must not be taken to the town."

"Eh, Condé woman! We have agreed to your other demands, but we might not be able to do this. What if we can't convince the people of Dò ni Kiri not to take the carcass back to town? What if they force us? We'll be powerless to fight them off or to take the carcass from them."

"Oh, you will do your best to heed what I have said. If you can do the other things, then forget about that last request. But you must respect my other two wishes."

"Very well."

As the brothers were about to leave, she said to them, "Sit down." Once they were sitting, she said, "The weapons you brought won't do anything to me. The arrows and quivers you brought won't do anything either. I am in control of my own life."

She put her hand in her basket of cleaned cotton, pulled out the spindle, and handed it to them. Then, putting her hand in her storage basket, she took out the distaff that usually holds the thread, and gave it to them, saying, "Put this in your bow and shoot the buffalo with it. It will stop the buffalo. If you do not shoot the buffalo with it—if you shoot a big arrow at the buffalo instead—then the buffalo will kill you."

[In an omitted passage, Dò Kamissa provides the brothers with various enchanted objects that will help them kill her buffalo wraith.]

DEATH OF THE BUFFALO

The brothers left the town and went into the bush, past the lake of Dò ni Kiri and into the forest. They crossed another open space and entered more forest. There, before going any further, they saw the buffalo.

(Before they came to the bush that day, the brothers' name was Sharifu. But afterwards they were called Diabaté or Tarawèlè. They left their Sharifu identity behind in Manden[53] and came to be known as Tarawèlè and Diabaté. We will soon come to the reason for this.)

There was the buffalo. Abdu Karimi, the younger brother, said to Abdu Kassimu, "Big brother! You should be the one to take the magic dart and shoot the buffalo, because the killing of this buffalo will make history. The person who kills this buffalo will be mentioned in all of the future generations' histories, right up until the trumpet is blown on Judgment Day. You are my big brother, so you kill the buffalo."

Abdu Kassimu said, "Little brother, a job must be left to the experts. Yes, I was the first to be born. But I know what *dalilu* you have—and I know you must be the one to kill the buffalo." He handed the magic dart to his younger brother.

Abdu Karimi told his elder brother to go on ahead. Crawling through the grass, Abdu Karimi came ever closer to the buffalo. He remembered what the old woman had told him: that he should not try to kill the buffalo until he was in its shadow. She'd said, "Do not miss me! If you miss the buffalo, I"ll kill you." The younger brother crawled until he reached the buffalo's shadow. He took the distaff and put it on the spindle. He pulled the string of his bow back, back, back, he

---

53. Only after the buffalo is mortally wounded does Tassey begin to use the names by which the brothers are usually known, Danmansa Wulanni and Danmansa Wulanba. These probably originated as praise names based on the brothers' exploits, e.g., Danmansa Wulanba can be roughly translated as "Big Lord of the Solitary Forest Buffalo" (for further details, see Major Characters).

pulled it still harder, and he could feel that he had something very powerful in his hand. When he'd pulled the bowstring back to his shoulder, he let the spindle go, *pow!* It shot right into the buffalo's chest.

The buffalo was startled when the spindle pierced its chest. It raised its head, saw Abdu Karimi, and bellowed, *hrrr!* And there, while he was still right beside the wounded buffalo, Abdu Karimi told his elder brother, "Run!" for the buffalo had been shot and the struggle between them had begun.

(It's said that greatness will not be acquired without hardship. We've been telling you about the hardship Manden had to endure before the country could know peace. Sunjata would not have been born without this hardship, and without Sunjata, Manden would never have been sweet. And if Manden was never sweet, we Mande people would never have known ourselves!)

Bellowing, the buffalo began to chase the *kamalenw*, it came up behind Abdu Karimi, who was trying to catch up with his elder brother. Abdu Karimi dropped the bamboo stick, which instantly sprouted into a grove of bamboo, and before the buffalo could get through it, the *kamalenw* were far ahead.

Once it was clear of the bamboo, the buffalo started chasing them again. When it came up behind them and bellowed, the brothers dropped the hot charcoal. In those days, the Mande bush had been there a long time and had never been burned. So when the *kamalenw* dropped the hot charcoal, the bush caught on fire, stopping the buffalo and forcing it back while they dashed ahead through the grass.

When the fire died out, the buffalo jumped into the ashes and started chasing them again. But by the time it reached them and bellowed, they were already at the lake of Dò ni Kiri. There Abdu Karimi dropped the egg, which turned the ground into deep mud. The buffalo got stuck in the mud. (This is the mud referred to in the, Condé song "Dala Kombo Kamba":

> "Condé drinker of big lake water,
> Those who drank the big lake water,
> They did not stop to clean it.

Those who clean the big lake,
They did not drink its big water."

It was Danmansa Wulanba and Danmansa Wulanni[54] who cleaned the water of the big lake.)

By the time the mud started to dry, it was too late for the buffalo: the spindle wounds were letting water into its intestines, and it fell down. When the buffalo fell, Danmansa Wulanni said, "Big brother, look behind you! The buffalo has fallen."

A new family lineage was created at the moment the elder brother looked back and saw that the buffalo was dying. Going back, he put his foot on the buffalo's body. He said, "Ah, little brother! You have given me a name. Ah, little brother! You were sired by Abdu Mutulu Budulaye, Abdu Mutulu Babatali. Aba Alibi's own son is Sedina Alia, to whom God gave a sword, and you were sired by Alia. Sedina Alia's son is Hassana Lonsani, and you were sired by him. Hassana Lonsani's son is Sissi; Sissi's son is Kèmo; Kèmo's son is Kèmomo Tènè; Kèmo Tènè's son is Sharifu—and you were sired by Sharifu. Aah, Karimi! You have given us names."

After hearing this praise, the younger brother said, "Eh, big brother! If you were a praise-singer or *jeli*, no one could surpass you (*i jèmba tè*)!"

That was the beginning of the *jeli* family known as Diabaté;[55] that was the origin of the lineage. "Diabaté" was first said in Manden, in the Mande language, when the buffalo was killed in the bush.

Once the buffalo was dead, the brothers saw that its tail was heavy with gold and silver.

---

54. The elder brother is Wulanba, the younger Wulanni.

55. The singing or chanting of praises is an occupational specialty of *jeliw*. This is a popular etymology (see n. 37) explaining how the Diabaté *jeliw* acquired their family name. When the younger brother killed the buffalo and the elder brother praised his courage by reciting their family genealogy, this was the way a *jeli* would do it. When the younger brother said, "no one could surpass you" the phrase *jèmba tè* evolved through repetition into "Diabaté" which, along with "Kouyaté" is one of the two names exclusive to traditional bards.

In cutting off the buffalo's tail, the brothers were able to take for themselves all of the gold and silver in its hair. The *kamalenw* were also able to use the tail as proof that they really had killed the buffalo. As soon as they showed the tail, people knew that the business was finished, because the tail of Dò Kamissa's buffalo wraith could only be cut off if the buffalo was dead. Ahuh! (And this was the beginning of the custom of removing the tails of dead game.)

[In an omitted passage, Danmansa Wulanba and Danmansa Wulanni try to respect Dò Kamissa's wish that her wraith be buried in the bush, but the townspeople insist on retrieving the buffalo carcass and dragging it into town to be desecrated.]

SOGOLON WULEN CONDÉ OF DÒ NI KIRI

After the buffalo was dead, the people of Dò ni Kiri started beating the ceremonial drum. All of the people living in the twelve towns of Dò, the four towns of Kiri, and the six towns across the river were expected to attend, and they all came. When the twenty-two towns were all present, the people said, "What did we say? We said that we'll bring out three age sets of girls for the hunter that kills this buffalo, and that he can choose any girl from among them to be his wife. Bring your daughters forward." (Huh! If you bring out three age sets of daughters from twenty-two towns, you should bring out the oldest set first, then the next oldest, then the youngest set.)

The villagers brought out the beautiful Condé girls, formed them into three circles, and told the boys to choose. The people said, "Even if you choose ten or twenty girls, they will be your wives. Or if you choose only one girl, she will be your wife. You have delivered us from disaster! And everyone here wants to have their daughters married to you two boys.

"You Sharifu, we don't go back on our promises. Take a look at these girls, and take any one that pleases you." The two men followed one another, walking around, around, around the circle. When they had returned to where they started they said, "Where are the rest of the girls?"

The Condé ancestor said, "You young men search every house, so that no one can hide his daughter."

The villagers searched the entire town but found no other girls. Everybody wanted to marry their daughter to the brothers!

When the searchers returned they said, "There is nobody left."

A bystander said, "What about the bad old woman who was just killed? She has her father's last-born still in her house."

Somebody said, "Eeh, man! Heeeye, can we show that one to the strangers?"

Danmansa Wulanni said, "Go and get that woman you're talking about. Has she been married to another man?"

They said, "No."

"Has she been married before?"

"No."

The brothers said, "Well, if she is unmarried, go get her."

The people said, "Out of five age sets of girls that have found husbands, only she has remained unmarried."

The brothers said, "If she is an unmarried girl, go get her."

Ma Dò Kamissa had told them that the door of Sogolon Wulen Condé's father's house was the one facing the town's meeting ground. She'd also told them, "When Sogolon is coming from my father's house to go into the town meeting ground, a little black cat will come from behind her and pass in front of her; the little black cat will go from in front of her and pass behind her. If you see that happening to anyone, then you'll know that she is the girl I am talking about."

They sent for Sogolon, and as she was being brought out of the house—just as she reached the edge of the town meeting ground—a black cat came from behind her and passed in front of her; it went from in front of her and passed behind her.

As soon as the brothers saw Sogolon, they said, "This is the one we've been talking about."

They heard people go, "Wooo!"

They were asked, "Is this really the one you were talking about?"

To which the brothers replied, "Yes, this is the one we have been talking about."

Ancestor Donsamogo Diarra said to them, "You Sharifu, is this the one you want?"

To which they replied, "Yes, this is the one we want."

"Are you *sure* this is the one you want?"

"This is the one we want."

He said, "This one is even more powerful than my sister, whom you killed, and you know how much *dalilu* she had. This one has *really* powerful *dalilu*. But if you say that you want her, I'll give her to you. Go ahead and take her with you. If you're not compatible, just bring her back. I'll return her to where you found her, and I'll give you another wife.

"Now, I don't want to contradict myself, but just take another look at these other girls. We'll give you up to three months. If, after three months, you're not compatible with my sister, come back and I will give you one of these girls. I will put my sister back where she came from."

The brothers said, "Very well."

She was Sogolon, the woman who was given to them, the mother of Simbon. Simbon, whose birth was foretold and who united Manden—this is the child about to be born. We can talk about Turama'an, we can talk about Kankejan, or of Tombonon Sitafa Diawara, of Fakoli, Sumaworo, or of Tabon Wana Faran Kamara; but the one who organized them all, united them into one place and called it Manden, well, the person who did all those things was Sunjata, and this is how his mother was married.

When the villagers gave Sogolon to them, Danmansa Wulanni, the younger brother, said, "This is my brother's wife. Give her to him."

When night falls and people go to bed, men normally get close to their brides. But when the elder brother, Danmansa Wulanba, got close to Sogolon, she did not accept his advances. She shot two porcupine quills from her chest and they stuck in him. He jumped up and fell on the ground. Afraid of her sorcery, he spent the rest of the night sleeping on the opposite side of the room.

In the morning when his little brother came to him, Danmansa Wulanba said, "Little brother, didn't I tell you yesterday that you should be the one to kill the buffalo?"

Danmansa Wulanni said, "Uh huh."

"Didn't I say that you know more than I do? Ahuh, you should marry this woman yourself. You'll just have to accept it. The God who made it possible for you to kill the buffalo has made me unable to take this woman. When we leave here, we'll exchange this gold and silver and I'll marry another woman who I will keep. Don't say anything to the Condé, so they cannot say '*wooo*' to us like they did yesterday. You take her without letting anybody here know about it."

That night Danmansa Wulanba was in a hurry for them to finish eating supper. When they were done, he took his blanket and went out to spend the night with his friends. By that time, Danmansa Wulanni and Sogolon Condé were in the house together. And when they went to bed, she did something really special to Danmansa Wulanni, something she hadn't done to his elder brother! It was so bad that where Danmansa Wulanba had spent the night on the other side of the room, Danmansa Wulanni slept outside the house.

The next morning, as soon as he saw his elder brother coming, Danmansa Wulanni said, "*Pah*! Big brother! I'm not going to say a thing to you. Let us beg to take our leave. There's no way that we can explain this. To think we rejected all those beautiful Condé women! Eh! The old woman has really caused problems for us. Eh! That old woman! She killed the men of Manden, but she sent us straight into decay. If we don't get another wife here, they will say we are too proud, that we look too high. We were given a group of women to choose from. We declined them, but can't keep the one we took. We shouldn't say that we don't want her. Let's just take our leave, and we'll abandon her by the side of the first flooded river we see. You and I will cross the river and go on; eventually she'll go back because she won't be able to cross."

The river was flooded when the boys arrived. Danmansa Wulanni said, "Sister-in-law, wait here for us. You can see the water yourself. We're going upstream, and if we find a tree that has fallen across the river, we'll come to get you so we can cross together."

Sogolon said, "All right," and waited for them there with her baggage. Everything was tied up in her bundle.

The brothers went farther and farther upstream until they saw a *sèbè* tree that had fallen across the river. Aah, the Sharifu now had their escape! They went across on the tree.

As they were crossing the river, Danmansa Wulanba said, "Eh heh, we have done the right thing. Don't you see how she attached herself to us? She would have just slowed us down. Who would want to take her along? Hey! Look at what she did to my chest."

Danmansa Wulanni said, "You don't even know what you're talking about. I won't even show you what she did to me. Sorceress! Who would want to marry a sorceress and bring her to his father's house?"

While they were chatting, they arrived at Konfara. There, at the outskirts of Konfara, they met the Condé woman sitting and waiting for them.

She said to them, "You Sharifu, is this how you behave?"

They said, "Ah, Ma, please forgive us."

A NEW SORCERESS WIFE FOR THE *MANSA* OF KONFARA

The Sharifu arrived in Konfara with Sogolon and went straight to Simbon's house. There Danmansa Wulanba said to Maghan Konfara, "You, ancestor of Nuru Soma,[56] Jidan Soma, Kalabali Soma, the first sorcerer of Manden and the last sorcerer of Manden; you, son of Latali Kalabi, Kalabi the younger and Kalabi the elder; you, whose fathers were Mamadi Kani and Kani Simbon, and Kani Nyogo Simbon, and Kabala Simbon, and Big Simbon Madi Tanyagati, and M'balinene, and Bele, and Belebakon, and Farako Manko Farakonken!

"I swear to God, you are a real king of diviners. What you told us is exactly what happened to us. We went to Dò ni Kiri, we killed the buffalo, the people of Dò ni Kiri honored us, and they gave us the woman you described. Because you foresaw all of this—and because of your forthrightness and the way you help travelers—we did not accept any other woman. We've brought you the woman you're looking for."

Simbon laughed. "Aheh, where is the woman in question?"

"She is outside."

Simbon got up, took his elephant-tail flywhisk, and looked around. He went and saw the sorceress sitting beside her bundle. As soon as he saw her, he said, "Heeee, Sharifulu, oh father! Take this one back. No, I'm not refusing her, I still want her. But take her out of the town and let me prepare myself. You brought me a gift that I want to keep. But if you bring her to my house right now, she will take it away from me. Go back outside the town." The brothers took Sogolon out of town and waited.

---

56. Danmansa Wulanba, now functioning as a *jeli*, begins to praise the *mansa* of Konfara, thus affirming his own identity as ancestor of the Diabaté lineage of bards.

Maghan Konfara gave ten kola[57] to Manjan Bereté (who became the first *karamogo* in Manden and worked to find the wife who would be Sunjata's mother) and said, "I have been given a wife; the Sharifu have brought me a wife. God has answered your prayers, Manjan Bereté, and granted your request. The Sharifu and the woman are still outside town. Go and meet them and welcome them into the town; tell them this is their home."

So Manjan Bereté took Sogolon Condé's ten marriage kola and used them to welcome the Sharifu. (If you ever see the Maninka carrying kola nuts like that, it means they are welcoming those who bring a bride. Sogolon Condé's were the first marriage kola of Manden, and the custom has been passed down through the generations.)

Manjan Bereté was happy to see the strangers. He said, "Karimi, Danmansa Wulanni, I give this kola to you and your brother to welcome you. Simbon says that the town is yours in return for the deeds you accomplished between Dò ni Kiri and Manden. Simbon says that you are welcome because you have freed us from the suffering and disaster brought upon the Condé at the hands of the sister's buffalo wraith. (For as long as your brother is suffering, you will also suffer.) You succeeded in killing the buffalo, and then returned to Manden with this special woman. Simbon is very pleased and says you are welcome. Heh! He says the town is yours and you should enter it now. He says the honor belongs to you and God, and has put me in charge of you strangers."

When the brothers had been thus honored, Manjan Bereté accompanied them to town.

(After the brothers gave Sogolon to Maghan Konfara, he took two of his daughters—the daughter known as Nana Triban, who had the same mother as Dankaran Tuman, and Tenenbajan, daughter of his younger brother—and gave them as wives to Danmansa Wulanni and Danmansa

---

57. Large, segmented, yellow, or red nuts containing caffeine, which are ritually sacrificed or presented upon—among other occasions—the arrival of a bride.

Wulanba, the men who had killed the buffalo. Nana Triban gave birth to Turama'an. Tenenbajan gave birth to Kankejan. These were the mothers of Turama'an and Kankejan, Danmansa Wulanni and Danmansa Wulanba's children.)

When the co-wives were told, "You have your wife,"[58] they took their places behind the bride. They said, "Sister-in-law, get up and let us go home." But when they lifted Sogolon up, they saw she had a twisted foot. Her feet were twisted, and she could not walk without stirring up dust. When the co-wives lifted her up, the dust went this way and that way.

Then they sang the first Mande song for welcoming brides. How did they sing this first bride-escorting song? The sisters sang:

> "Walk well,
> Bride of my brother,
> Walk well.
> Do not put us in the dust."

That became the first bride-escorting song of Manden.

Because they saw that Sogolon was walking as well as she could, and that walking any better was beyond her power, the sisters said, "Let us carry her." (This is how the tradition began of having women run into town carrying a bride. It started with the condition of Sogolon Condé's feet!)

At that time the men in a family were not considered to be the closest relatives; the women in a family were closer. As the co-wives carried Sogolon, they saw other women on the road. And if those women had not shouted encouragement, the co-wives would never have arrived at their destination. They were, after all, carrying a mature woman. Five age sets of Condé women had found husbands—but she had not been married. Yes, she was a very mature woman.

The sisters then said, "Don't you see the horse?"

---

58. The bride is thought of as the collective possession of the family and the village into which she marries.

The co-wives looked back and said, "Which horse do you mean?"

"The Horse of Manden."

And before the co-wives could turn around, the sisters were already running past them saying, "You're carrying the Horse of Manden!"

While they were running, Ma Sogolon Condé's headscarf fell off, and her bald head was exposed. The co-wives, who had not known that she was bald, made a new song. What did the co-wives sing? They sang:

> "The heron-head oooh.
> Our heron-head has come this year,
> Heron-head.
> The woman's heron-head has come this year with her crest."

This offended Sogolon Condé. She looked back at the women of Manden and said, "Are you calling me a heron-head? Huh! Am I the one you are calling heron-head? Well, I have arrived."

Feeling angry, she was carried to her new husband's door. Her husband had been sitting in his lounge chair at the back of his room, and had prepared himself with his own *dabali*.[59] He had taken out his sorcerer's whip and laid it at his side, because he knew that the woman coming to him would show him her *dalilu*.

The first time the co-wives tried to push Sogolon inside to her husband, they held the back of her head. But she shot a sorcerer's dart from her eye and tried to pierce her husband's eye. The dart went *srrrrr*!

Maghan Konfara caught it. He said, "Condé woman, you have brought me a present. This is the seventh year that I have had the meat of Mande sorcery in my teeth. An ordinary piece of straw will not be able to pick it from my teeth; only a sorcerer's dart will do that. You have brought me a dart for a

---

59. A scheme or plan (pl. *dabaliw*); as a verb, the secret power sometimes associated with evil (see Glossary).

toothpick." He caught the dart and laid it beside him. Then he took his sorcerer's whip and lashed her on the head, *cho*!

Sogolon pulled back for the first time. When she put her head in again, she shot out her scalding breast milk, trying to splash it on Simbon to blister his skin, to let him know that a real woman was coming.

Simbon repelled it. He said, "Condé woman, you have really brought me a gift. Ordinary Mande water does not clean our faces as well as warm breast milk. You have brought me face-washing water." He washed his face with the breast milk and again picked up his sorcerer's whip. He lashed her on the head, *cho*! She pulled back her head a second time.

The third time when the women tried to push her in, Sogolon took out a staff with a small metal point on the end and tried to spear Simbon in the chest with it, because she could see she was up against a real man. (Sometimes you'll see old men of Manden carrying such a staff; it was Sogolon Condé who brought it from Dò ni Kiri. It belongs to the Condé.) Sogolon had thrown two things at Maghan Konfara, and both had been repelled. If this one worked, it would pierce his chest. But when Sogolon threw the staff, Simbon merely caught it and praised it.

He said, "We walk with the *sunsun* stick with nothing on it, but the Condé have sent us a *sunsun* stick wearing a hat."[60] (That is the staff in question. It was not an ordinary spear; it was his new bride's spear.) Simbon said, "We have received a protective spear." He laid it beside him, picked up his sorcerer's whip, and lashed her, *cho*!

(These days, when a Mande bride arrives at her husband's door, her sisters will put their heads in the room and then pull them back out, put their heads inside and pull them back out. After doing this three times, they send the bride in to her husband. This tradition started with Sogolon and her husband.)

Sogolon had used up her sorcery. The co-wives pushed her in to Maghan Konfara. Once she was inside with him,

---

60. A metaphorical reference to the staff's metal tip.

she reached for her bundle and took out her drinking ladle. Sogolon Condé was the first to put into water the ten kola nuts that are usually given to a bride. She was told to put them into the water instead of handing them to her husband, so she put them in her cup and knelt in front of Maghan Konfara. (Nowadays, it's the woman who is supposed to put the kola in water and then hand it to her husband. But back then many people were asking to do it.)

She said, "You, Latali Kalabi, Kalabi Doman, and Kalabi Bomba, God and Mamadi Kani. God and Kani Simbon, God and Kani Nyogo Simbon, God and Kabala Simbon. God and Big Simbon Madi Tanyagati. God and M'balinene, God and Bele and Belebakon, God and Farako Manko Farakonken. If you were not among the husbands of the world, I would have gone to the other world unmarried. Now I have come to my husband. He is my married husband, my husband who will take care of me, the husband by whom I will give birth. I have received my husband. 'It is the crocodile of the stream that leads one to the crocodile of the river.' I have come to Simbon. Drink." Simbon drank.

Maghan Konfara accepted the ten kola nuts from Sogolon and set them down. They were finished with the sorcery. Alone, Sogolon went and sat on her husband's bed. (If you see a new bride sitting in a chair instead of her husband's bed, she has something on her mind. She does not want to marry this man; she has another man's name to confess. It is good for a new bride to want to be with her husband.)

Sitting on the bed, Sogolon said, "The women called me heron-head. I have not forgotten that."

But the women of Manden only wanted to have fun. Ah, *gba*! Big sister, Jelimuso Tunku Manyan Diawara, Jonmusoni Manyan, Tassisi Gbandimina, Maramajan Tarawelé, and Mama Damba Magasuba said, "Who could be jealous of such a person? It is better to compete with one's equal. She is bald-headed, she has a humped back, she has a weeping tear duct, and her feet are twisted. Why should we be jealous of this woman? Let's welcome her to begin with. Let's tell the men of Manden that each of us will have a day to cook for the strangers." (This is why the Mande bride-welcoming ceremony lasts for eight days.) Each of those women chose her day to cook, and each killed a chicken.

On the eighth day, the men of the town said, "Eh! Why should we just sit here watching our women get all the recognition? We men must seize this day for ourselves. If the women have killed chickens, we'll kill a goat." (This is why we slaughter a goat for a wedding; this was the first "day of killing a stranger's goat.")

When the celebration was at its peak, the bridal drum was played in the town circle. The celebration with the bridal drum outdid the celebration of circumcision. When the party reached the town circle, all the women were there in force.

Sogolon Condé said to her husband, "Simbon, if you agree, I would like to watch the people as they dance for the bride in the town circle."

Maghan Konfara said, "Eh! Condé woman, that might be what they do in Dò ni Kiri, the home of the Condé, but here in Manden, women do not attend the bride's dance circle."

"Un un, I will not go in person. If you agree, I'll stay here behind you but still watch them in the circle." She wanted to use her sorcery. (This one night caused Sogolon's seven-year pregnancy and kept Sunjata from walking once he was born.)

Simbon said, "Ah, if you won't go there in person, then there's no reason for us to argue. There is no sorcery you can show me that could be worse than that with which you started. If you keep your body here but can still see them, I will not say 'no.'"

"Very well."

Lying behind her husband on the bed, Sogolon put her left hand on him. She stretched out her right arm and her right hand passed through the straw roof. She stretched her arm to reach the dance circle and laid her hand up in the *dubalen* tree. She pointed two fingers down; light came out of them. The circle was suddenly full of light, *wa*! And she was still lying behind her husband.

From behind her husband she said, "Heeeh, Mande people know how to do it. Heeeh, Jonmusoni Manyan really knows how to dance! Heeeh, Tunku Manyan Diawara has a good voice! Heeh, Tassisi Gbandimina knows how to dance! Heeh, Maramajan Tarawèlè is dancing! Heeh, Flaba Naabi, heeya, she knows!"

While the women were dancing, Jonmusoni Manyan raised her head. When she saw that the inner circle was all lit up, even though there were no torches, she looked up and saw the two fingers hanging down. They were giving off light like a pressure lamp. She said, "Big sister Sansun Bereté, Big sister Maramajan Tarawèlè, lift up your eyes. This is the one of whom we said we wouldn't need to be jealous. This is a sprouting tree,[61] and when it grows to extend its branches, it will take Manden away from us. Hee! The new bride is lying behind her husband, but she's watching us with her two fingers, look! Do you see the two fingers with eyes? Mande women, if you are real women, you'd better get ready. This one must not be successful here."

The wedding dance stopped suddenly. Feeling chilled, all the women went home, where they dipped their hands into their *dalilu.*

Sogolon was still a virgin when she came to Maghan Konfara. After three days, her bloody virgin cloth was taken out. The following month, she became pregnant with Sunjata. That is how Sunjata was conceived.

The co-wives said, "We won't be able to do anything against this woman." She had gone to her husband almost at the end of the lunar month, and for the rest of that month, she did not see the other moon. She had conceived.

When the women of Manden heard this, they went outside the town and held a meeting under a baobab tree. They said, "Getting pregnant is one thing, delivering is another. Make miscarriage medicine, anything that will spoil the belly with a touch. Everyone must prepare her own."

Sogolon Condé also had very powerful *dalilu.* When her belly started to expand, the other wives would visit her, saying, "Younger sister, this is the medicine we use here in

---

61. A metaphorical allusion to Sogolon.

Manden for pregnant women. Aah, all of the women here wanted a child, but we have not been able to conceive. You may be the lucky one bearing our husband's child—but the child belongs to all of us. Here, M'ma, dilute this medicine in water and drink it."

Heh, Sogolon, the Condé woman, diluted that medicine in water and drank it. She drank it and drank it, for seven years. And each time she drank it, her belly would shrink away, *jè!*

After seven years of this, Sogolon Condé went outside the town.

She prayed to God. She said, "M'mari! That is enough! Enough of what those Mande people have done to me. I come to you, God. I am only a stranger here, and the men who brought me here cannot help."

[In an omitted passage, the narrator describes his own family's relationship with characters in the narrative, and with ancestors from Arab tradition.]

THE CHILDHOOD OF MA'AN SUNJATA

God made Ma'an Sunjata into a person, made him into a human fetus and brought him into the world.

When the Mande women heard the news of Ma'an Sunjata's birth, they again gathered together under the Mande baobab tree. They said, "It is one thing to give birth to a son, but another thing for him to survive."

Then what did they do to him? Through sorcery they stretched the tendons of his two feet. They lamed him and forced him to crawl on the ground for one year!

Two years!

Three years!

Four years!

Five years!

Six years!

Then, in Sunjata's seventh year, the co-wives provoked Sogolon to anger. (Because we are walking on a straight path, we cannot wander from one side to the other. We have to take the main road, so we will know how Manden was built.)

One day, in Sunjata's seventh year, Maramajan Tarawèlè was picking some leaves from the same baobab tree that we've already mentioned. As Maramajan Tarawèlè was on her way back to the villiage, Ma Sogolon Wulen Condé, who was sitting under the eaves of the house she shared with Ma'an Sunjata, asked, "Big sister Maramajan Tarawèlè, won't you give me a few of your baobab leaves?"

Maramajan Tarawèlè said, "Ah! Younger sister, you are the only one of us to have a son. Why would you ask us for baobab leaves? Your lame son is sitting right there inside the house. If you want baobab leaves, why don't you tell your son to stand up and go get some?"

Ma Sogolon Wulen Condé said, "Ah, that is not what I meant. I thought I could depend on the help of my sisters. I didn't know you were upset because I had this child."

The two women didn't know Sunjata was listening to them.

Afterwards, when Ma Sogolon Condé walked by, Sunjata said, "Mother! Mother!" She did not answer because she knew he had overheard them.

He said, "Mother, what are they saying?"

"Forget about that talk."

"Ah, how can I ignore that? Mother, I'll walk today. They insult you by saying you have a lame person in your house, and yet you beg them for a baobab leaf? I'll walk today. Go and get my father's *sunsun* staff, and bring it to me. I'll walk today."

Ma Sogolon Condé went and got the *sunsun* staff and brought it to Simbon. When he attempted to stand by thrusting the *sunsun* staff firmly into the ground and holding on to it, the *sunsun* staff broke.

Sunjata said to Sogolon, "Ah, mother. They say you have a lame son in the house, but you gave birth to a real son. Nothing happens before its time. Go and bring my father's iron staff." But when she gave him the iron staff, he broke it, too.

He said, "Go and tell my father's blacksmith to forge an iron staff so I can walk." The blacksmith carried one load of iron to the bellows, forged it, and made it into an iron staff. But when Sunjata thrust that iron staff into the ground and tried to stand, the staff bent. (That iron staff, the one they say was bent by Sunjata into a bow, is now in Narena.)

Sunjata broke both of his father's staffs and an iron one that was forged for him. Therefore, when he stood, he did it on his own, first lifting one foot, then the other foot, then the other one, and so on.

His mother said, "Simbon has walked!"

The *jeliw* sang this song:

> "Has walked,
> Jata has walked.
> Has walked,
> Jata has walked."

Thus it was his mother's rivalry with her co-wives, and their humiliation of her, that caused Jata to walk. (That is why I can't believe it when I hear people saying they do not love their mother! Heh! Jelimori![62] Your father belongs to everyone, but your mother belongs only to you. When you meet people for the first time, they don't ask you about your father; they ask about your mother.)

After that, God gave Sunjata feet. Sunjata went into the house, took his father's bow and quiver, and left town. (Some

---

62. During performances, *jeliw* occasionally speak to people in the audience, commenting on something in the narrative.

people say he made the bent iron staff into his bow, but don't repeat that.)[63]

When he reached the baobab tree, he shook it, uprooted it, and put it on his shoulder. He carried it into his mother's yard and said, "Now everyone will come here for baobab leaves."

So it was that when the Mande women next saw Sogolon they said, as they picked the baobab leaves, "Aah, Sogolon Condé! We knew this would happen for you. The prayers and sacrifices we made on your behalf have been answered." (Now, when you are having a hard time, everyone abuses you. But when things are going well for you, people say, "We knew this would happen for you." May God help us persevere!)

Sogolon eventually had three more children. After So'olon Ma'an[64] was born—but before he could walk—his younger brother So'olon Jamori was born. Then, while So'olon Ma'an was still crawling on the ground, Manden Bori was born. Finally after So'olon Ma'an walked, So'olon Kolonkan was born.

STEP-BROTHER RIVALRY AND NINE SORCERESSES OF MANDEN

[In omitted passages, Sunjata and his brothers assure their half-brother Dankaran Tuman that as long as he lives, his right to

---

63. The bard himself does not believe that part of the legend.

64. Sogolon's Maghan (*maghan* = "king," "lord"), one of several praise-names by which the *jeliw* refer to Sunjata.

*their father's legacy will be uncontested. The narrator describes
the non-Mande origins of Sumaworo's father, how he acquired his
wives, including Sumaworo's mother, and how Sumaworo became
a hunting apprentice to Sunjata's father. The four provinces of
Soso are introduced, and the boundary between them and Manden is described. Dankaran Tuman quarrels with his mother, Sansun Bereté, and they conspire to have Sunjata murdered by a coven
of nine sorceresses, but one of them comes to warn him.]*

Jelimusoni Tunku Manyan Diawara, one of the nine sorceresses, was Sunjata's ally. She came to Simbon in the middle of the night and told him about their plan.

She said, "Sunjata, if God agrees with our plan, we'll
kill you the day after tomorrow. You'd better do something to protect yourself. Among the cows from your
father's legacy (the ones you declined to take from your
brother) is a big bull. Dankaran Tuman has told us—big
sister Tasissi Gbandimina, Jonmusoni Manyan, Jelimusoni
Tunku Manyan Diawara, Nyuma Danba Magasuba, Maramajan Tarawèlè, and me—that if we kill you, he'll give
us that bull. Because we crave meat we have agreed to use
our sorcery to do this.

"Watch out for yourself. You should do something about
this; talk to them and tell them you'll make it worth their
while to spare your life. Otherwise, we'll kill you the day after
tomorrow, while you are hunting in the bush. I know hunting
is very important to you, but if you go out we'll kill you. You
are no match for us."

Sunjata took her hand and said, "Thank you for telling
me the truth. Very well, go and tell them that they must
spare me, as I am the son of a Condé woman. Tell them that
one bull is not bigger than three male antelope, and that if
they spare me, I will give them three male antelope for the
one bull. Tell them to spare me; they should not do what my
brother asks."

When Jelimusoni Tunku Manyan Diawara told this to the sorceresses, they said, "All we want is meat. Tell Sunjata that if he does what he has said, he will have no problem."

That night and the next day passed. When the *sigbé* bird chirped at the break of the following dawn, Simbon put on his crocodile-mouth hat,[65] hung his hunter's whistle on his chest, took his hammock, quiver, and bow, and left the town.

When he was one kilometer outside of town, he saw an antelope. He shot at it and knocked it down. He shot another arrow, hit another antelope, and knocked it down. He shot still another arrow, and the sun had not even turned white before he'd killed three antelope.

(God sides with the just. A man can decide what he wants to do with his life, but it is God who makes the final decision! The chick destined to be a rooster will eventually crow, no matter what obstacles it has to overcome before it can do so.)

On his way back, Sunjata left the three antelope he'd killed at the edge of town. He told Jelimusoni Tunku Manyan Diawara that she should tell the other sorceresses that their meat was at the edge of town.

Upon hearing this, the sorceresses set out to find the game. They butchered the antelope; they roasted some of the meat, they boiled some of it, they fried some of it, and made some of it into meatballs. Afterwards they said, "Ma'an Sunjata, no female genie will harm you, let alone a human female."

(What had saved him? His hands. When you are popular, you must have an open hand. A man's generosity will save him from those that mean him harm.)

The sorceresses blessed him. They said, "We are with you to the death. No female will ever harm you: no female genie will chase you, no female ant will ever sting you, no female wild animal will ever hurt you. We promise this, God willing, or we are not producers of kitchen smoke."

Thus they spared him.

---

65. Maninka *bamada*: a distinctive, cone-shaped hat with flaps at the front and back.

MISTAKEN MURDER AND
THE QUESTION OF EXILE

*[In an omitted passage, Dankaran Tuman and his mother con-
spire to have Sunjata murdered in his sleep. Meanwhile, Sunjata
spends a rainy day playing the hunter's harp while he waits for the
weather to change so he can go hunting.]*

As So'olon Ma'an waited for the rain to stop so he could
go hunting, he sat in his hammock with his six-stringed hunter's harp and sang to himself. (His younger brothers Manden Bori and So'olon Jamori were also harp players.) After
playing "Kulanjan"[66] for a while, Sunjata changed tunes and
played "Sori."[67]

Some youths passing by So'olon Ma'an's door heard him
singing in a low, sweet voice and stopped in his door to listen.
One of these youths was an apprentice hunter. He said, "I will
listen to Sunjata until the rain stops."

While the youth stood at the door, Sunjata put some snuff
into his mouth. When the snuff was wet, he stopped playing
the harp and went to spit out the door, where he noticed the
young man. Sunjata said, "Who's there?"

The youth said, "Brother So'olon Ma'an, it is me."

"Ah, what are you doing here?"

"Your brother sent a message that we should bring him
some food and supplies. So that's what I'm doing. But it
is raining, and a slave with wet clothes does not enter the
house of his betters. I am an apprentice hunter at the farm.

---

66. One of the oldest melodies in the bards' repertory; often dedicated
to hunters, Sumaworo is praised as "Kulanjan."

67. A lesser-known melody dedicated to hunters.

I stopped under your eaves when I heard your music. Let me keep listening to you until the rain stops."

(Meanwhile, the musket[68] of conspiracy was being loaded in town.)

So'olon Ma'an said to the youth, "Come into the house."

The young man entered the house and sat on the edge of the bed. Simbon was playing the harp. When he played certain parts, the young man would tap his feet, because the harp music was so sweet. But the youth was also tired, and the warm room felt good to him. He became sleepy and started to nod. Ma'an Sunjata told him, "Lie on the bed." When the young man was asleep on the bed, Simbon stood up and covered the young man with a blanket. When the rain stopped, Sunjata—who forgot about the young man sleeping there—stood up, put on his crocodile-mouth hat, took his hunter's hammock, his quiver, bow, and fly whisk,[69] shut the front door, and went out the back. Taking a deep breath, he went into the bush.

While Simbon was in the bush, Dankaran Tuman came and stood under the eaves of the house, where he heard the young man snoring. He did not know that Ma'an Sunjata had left the house.

Dankaran Tuman went and told the seven young men, "Didn't I tell you that Sunjata sleeps any time it rains into the evening? He's sleeping now; go get your clubs."

After getting their clubs, the seven young men came to Simbon's door. But they were afraid of him. To each other they said, "Man, don't you know who So'olon Ma'an is? One man can't outdo him, two men can't outdo him, even the

---

68. Maninka *morifa*. The first firearms did not arrive in West Africa until the 16th century, but the *jeliw* frequently speak of muskets in the time of Sunjata. Linear chronology is not a pressing issue in their views of the distant past, but what is of interest is the imagery of a formidable weapon and a hero's power to repel any iron projectile.

69. Ideally made from the tail of a dangerous wild animal and possibly symbolizing the one cut from the slain Buffalo of Dò, although elephant tails were highly prized for this essential hunters' device carrying occult protective qualities.

seven of us together can't outdo him. When we go in, listen
carefully for the sound of his breathing, and be sure to hit
him on the head. If we only hit him on the back, he'll be sure
to capture us." They went in and surrounded the young man.
When they located the source of his breathing, they raised
their clubs and hit him on the head. They beat him until his
body went cold.

When the body was cold, they left to tell Dankaran Tuman
that they'd finished the work he had given them. Dankaran
Tuman told his mother, "Ahah, Mother. The bad thing is now
off our backs. He is dead." (No matter how good you think
you are, you'll always do something bad to your enemy!)

"Eh! Dankaran Tuman," she said, "has he died?"

"Yes! The son of the Condé woman has died today!"

"Ah, my son! Now I will not be the failure in my husband's
home. Now my heart is cool. If you have killed Ma'an Sunjata,
aagba! Manden Bori and So'olon Jamori can't stand up to
you. The only brother I was worried about has been killed."

They did not sleep that night.

Sansun Bereté said, "Heee, just wait until Sogolon Condé
knows about this."

When day broke, Dankaran Tuman and his mother went
to spy on Sogolon.

"Huh!" they whispered. "Don't say or do anything! When
he's slept for a long time, his mother will go and open the
door on him."

Sansun Bereté said, "If you don't say anything, no one will
guess that you are the one who killed him."

As the soft morning sun rose on them, they saw Sunjata,
Danama Yirindi[70]—yes, the son of the Condé woman—walking along, carrying three dead animals; one was hanging over
his left shoulder, one was hanging over his right shoulder,
and one was on his head.

When they saw him, Sansun Bereté said, "Dankaran
Tuman! Didn't you say that Sunjata was dead?"

Dankaran Tuman replied, "Mother, we really killed him."

---

70. A praise-name for Sunjata that can be translated as "superhero."

"Then who is this coming? Who is coming?"

"It is Sunjata who is coming."

When they saw that it really was Sunjata, Dankaran Tuman peed in his pants.

Walking up to them, Sunjata said to Sansun Bereté, "Big mother, here is some wild game for you." Then, laying another animal before his step-brother, he said, "Big brother, here is one for you."

There was nothing they could say.

Sunjata carried the last animal to his mother's place and said, "Mother, here is your animal."

His mother said, "Ah, my son, thank you."

When he returned to his house and pushed the door open, there were flies all over the stinking body—wooooo!

Sunjata shouted, "Mother, Mother! Come here! I'll kill someone today. Ever since I was born, I've never done anything bad like this. My brother did this, and I'll take revenge."

Ma Sogolon Condé came to the door.

Sunjata said, "You see this? I went to the bush and forgot about the young man you see lying here. My brother's men beat him to death with their clubs. I'll kill for this young man. I know this is Dankaran Tuman's boy, but he died my death. I'll prove to them that I am not the one who died."

Ma Sogolon Condé knew that Konfara would be destroyed by So'olon Ma'an's revenge, because he would kill anyone known to be one of Dankaran Tuman's supporters.

Sunjata dashed out of the house. When he reached for his iron staff, his mother ran and called Jelimusoni Tunku Manyan Diawara.

Sogolon said, "Sunjata is going to kill someone right now if you don't stop him."

Jelimusoni Tunku Manyan Diawara went and took hold of Simbon.

She said, "Simbon, won't you think about your mother? Simbon! Won't you think of me? Won't you leave this to God? Don't you realize that Dankaran Tuman has poked himself in the eye?" Sunjata tried and tried to break away, but she would not let go. Ha! She was able to hold him.

Then Ma Sogolon Condé said, "My son Sunjata, your popularity is your biggest problem. If they have started murdering people because of you, shouldn't we go away?"

This is why they went into exile. (One never sells his father's homeland, but it can be pawned!)

DEPARTURE FOR EXILE

[In an omitted passage, Sunjata repeatedly refuses to flee from his step-brother, but Sogolon argues that neither he nor Dankaran Tuman can understand the special circumstances of her background in Dò ni Kiri and how she was brought to their father because of Sunjata's destiny. She convinces Sunjata that even if they go away, he will eventually take over the leadership of Manden.]

Ma Sogolon Condé then set out to visit Sansamba Sagado, the Somono[71] ancestor. (This is the Sansamba Sagado you always hear about in the histories of Manden. He was involved with the organization of Manden, and those towns along the bank of the river—Jelibakoro, Sansando, and Baladugu—are populated with his Mande descendants. If you talk about Manden without talking about Sansamba Sagado, you have not covered the subject of Manden.)

Saying, "Sansamba Sagado," Sogolon removed her silver wrist and ankle bracelets and gave them to the Somono ancestor as the price for a future river crossing. This way, he would take her children across the river whenever they

---

71. Maninka- or Bamana-speaking specialists in fishing, canoeing, boating, and the water-borne transport of people and goods.

needed to cross, at any time of day or night, without anybody in Manden knowing that he'd done so.

The days passed. Then, one day, at three o'clock in the morning, Sogolon woke up her children and said, "The time has come for what we talked about."

They left together. When they came to the riverbank, she took the path to Sansamba Sagado's house. Waking him, she said, "This is the day we talked about."

He was not a man to break his promise. Taking his bamboo pole and his paddle, he left to meet Sogolon and her children in the bushes by the bank of the river. The water was rising; it nearly touched the leaves on the bushes. Sansamba Sagado's canoe was attached to a *npeku* tree; he untied it and brought it to them, saying, "Get in!"

Ma Sogolon Condé, her daughter Ma Kolonkan, Manden Bori, and So'olon Jamori got into the canoe. But when they told Sunjata to get in, he refused.

Ma Sogolon Condé said, "Ah, Sunjata! Do you want to make me suffer?"

He said, "Mother, if I told you that I will go with you, then I will go. You take the canoe now; I will join you later."

They crossed the river in the canoe, and before they could reach the other side, they saw Sunjata sitting on the bank. He had brought his *dalilu* with him.

A VISIT TO SOSO

[In an omitted passage, Sogolon decides to stop in Soso to ask for the help of Sumaworo, a powerful sorcerer who, in his youth, had been her husband's hunting apprentice. Meanwhile, Sumaworo's personal oracle informs him that the man who will eventually take

Soso and Manden away from him has not only been born, but has grown up into a hunter and will be identifiable as the one who violates Sumaworo's taboo.]

They were now in Soso.

Sogolon Condé arrived and said, "Eh, Soso *mansa.* These are the children of your former master. Their relationship with their brother is strained, and murder has been committed as a result. The death of one of two friends[72] does not spoil the friendship; the one who survives continues the friendship. I've come to put Ma'an Sunjata and his younger siblings under your protection. You should train them to be hunters, people who can kill their own game." (Oh! She did not know that Dankaran Tuman had sent a message ahead of them to Soso!)[73]

Sumaworo said, "Condé woman, that pleases me. I agree to care for them and take them under my protection, so long as they do not interfere with my sacred totem."

"God willing, they will never spoil your totem."

"Well, if they do not interfere with my totem, then I agree to protect them."

They spent the day there. That evening Ma Sogolon Condé said that she had brought a small amount of cotton she wanted to spin at night, and asked the children of Soso to collect a pile of dried cow dung she could use to light her lantern of conversation.[74] The children brought her the cow dung she needed. Sumaworo owned all the musical instruments, and he brought all of them—except for the *bala*—out for the first time that night. He brought out the *kèrèlèngkèngbèng,*[75]

---

72. Sumaworo and Sunjata's father.

73. Offering a reward to kill Sunjata.

74. When villagers gather after dark to socialize and play music, they do it around a lantern to avoid burning valuable fuel needed for cooking fires.

75. Named from the sound it makes (i.e., onomatopoeic), this child's instrument consists of a tin can resonator (or a tiny gourd) and a stick for a neck that supports a single string.

the *kòwòro*,[76] the *donso nkoni*,[77] the three-stringed *bolon*,[78] the *soron*,[79] and the *kora*.[80] (The *kora* was the last of the instruments to be brought out; that is why they call it *ko la*, which means "the last one."[81] Eventually it came to be called *kora*. It is played in Kita and Senegal.)

Taking out his *nkoni*,[82] Sumaworo sat down by the people who were talking. Sunjata and his siblings came and sat down too. Contented, Ma Sogolon Condé said, "Wait. I will sing three songs." They said, "Very well." When anybody sang, Sumaworo would accompany them on the *nkoni*.

For Ma Sogolon Condé's first song, she sang:

> "Big ram,
> The pen where the rams are kept,
> The leopard must not enter,
> Big ram.
> The pen where the rams are kept,
> The leopard must not enter."

Sumaworo's *nkoni* was in harmony with her song.
After that, what else did she sing? She sang:

> "Pit water,
> Don't compare yourself with clear water flowing over
> rocks,

---

76. More commonly known as *dan*, an inverted open calabash instrument with a neck for each of its six strings; technically known as a pentatonic pluriac.

77. The hunters' harp, a large animal-skin-covered calabash with a single neck and six strings, played to praise hunters.

78. The harp used to praise warriors; larger and deeper toned than the hunters' harp, an animal-skin-covered calabash with a single neck supporting three or four strings.

79. A large, rarely seen harp of northeastern Guinea, similar to the *kora* but with twelve strings.

80. With twenty-one strings, the largest of the calabash harps.

81. *Ko la* = literally "later on," another popular etymology (see n. 55).

82. Bamana *ngoni*; a traditional lute consisting of four to five strings attached to a single neck on a wooden, trough-shaped body covered with animal skin.

The pure white rocks.
Pit water,
Don't compare yourself with clear water flowing over
rocks,
The pure white rocks."

Again, Sumaworo's *nkoni* was in harmony with her song.
The third song she sang was:

"Big vicious dog,
If you kill your vicious dog,
Somebody else's will bite you,
Vicious dog.
If you kill your vicious dog,
Somebody else's will bite you."

Sumaworo's *nkoni* was still in harmony with her song.
Then the gathering broke up.

*[In omitted passages, Sumaworo performs a ritual to identify his
rival for power, learns that it is Sunjata, and resolves to kill him.
Sunjata intentionally violates a taboo by sitting in Sumaworo's
sacred hammock, confirming that he is the rival described by the
oracle. In an episode about Sumaworo's youthful rebelliousness
and leadership, he invents different stringed musical instruments
at various stages of his youth.]*

THE BIRTH OF FAKOLI

[The narrator recites Fakoli's genealogy and claims that his ances-tors in the male line had only one son each.]

Fakoli was an only son.

How was Fakoli born? The first wife of Yerelenko, Fakoli's father, was Tenenba Condé. Yerelenko married Tenenba Condé at the home of the Condé in Dò ni Kiri. Having gone thirty years without getting pregnant, Tenenba Condé told her husband, "I will never bear a child. I now have grey in my hair, and your beard is grizzled. You should marry another woman, so she can bear you a son."

Yerelenko said, "Tenenba Condé, I am not going to marry another wife. People were made for domestic strife; if I had many wives, they would just cause problems for you. If a man's second wife does not get along with his first wife, it makes him miserable. I will not take another wife. If you do not bear a child, you can care for me as if I were a child."

Ma Tenenba Condé wept and went to see her husband's friends. Still weeping, she said, "Please tell my husband to marry another woman. It is important to have a child. Whether it is a son, whether it is a daughter, whether it dies or survives, it is important to have a child. I will be held responsible if this continues and he dies without a child."

Yerelenko finally agreed to take another wife, and went to Soso to see Sumaworo. Sumaworo's younger sister was Kosiya Kanté. When she was old enough to leave home, Yerelenko married her. He paid the bride price for her, he waited for her, and eventually she became pregnant. After she got pregnant, she gave birth to a son.

Fakoli was Kosiya Kanté's son. This is the Fakoli you've heard about, the one who did right by the Mande people. He did not help Manden with a sword, or a musket; Fakoli helped Manden with the battle-axe he carried on his shoulder. Fakoli, the son of Kosiya Kanté, had a battle-axe.

(If you hear someone say, "I missed him," it means they were aiming a gun. A gun might miss you, a sword might miss you, but not a battle-axe. That one will not miss you.)

HOW TENENBA ACQUIRED FAKOLI: SUMAWORO'S QUEST FOR THE SOSO BALA

Sometimes you hear people refer to Fakoli as "Soma Tenenba's son." But if Kosiya Kanté gave birth to Fakoli, how did Soma Tenenba become his "mother"?

When Fakoli was a toddler being carried on the back of Kosiya Kanté—around the time he was beginning to walk, but before he was steady on the ground—Sumaworo was a young man completing his hunting apprenticeship. One day, while young Sumaworo was in the bush of Soso, a Folonengbe genie from Kodowari[83] named Jinna Maghan, who had long hair down his back,[84] appeared before him. Sumaworo followed Jinna Maghan all night through the bush of Soso and Manden, all the way to Folonengbe. Upon reaching the edge of Folonengbe, Jinna Maghan entered a cave, and it

---

83. Maninka pronunciation of Côte d'Ivoire, referring to a forested region in the northern part of what foreign traders called the "Ivory Coast," lying adjacent to today's eastern Guinea.

84. As supernatural beings, genies are perceived by Manding peoples in a variety of physical manifestations. Jinna Maghan (*jinna* = genie; *maghan* = king/chief) is ubiquitous, conjured by the bards wherever they wish to place him in their narratives.

was there, just at the entrance to the cave, that Sumaworo became a man. Sumaworo could transform himself into anything that flies through the air or walks on the ground. He could become the air itself and rise into the sky; he could also become anything on the ground.[85]

He was in strange, unfamiliar bush: he was not in the bush of Manden, Soso, Dò ni Kiri, or Folonengbe.[86] Raising his eyes, he saw a big *siri* tree standing by the entrance to the cave. It had some ripe fruit on it. He climbed into the tree, saying, "M'ba, let me hang my hunter's hammock here until daybreak. If the animals come to eat the ripe *siri* seeds, I'll have a shot at them." (It is animals that bring trouble to hunters.)

It was not an animal but a defining moment that arrived while he was lying in the tree. Jinna Maghan came out of the cave, which was all lit up in the night, and stood in the entrance looking around. Up in the tree, Sumaworo was not afraid, for God had removed all fear from him. The genie chief then brought out two young male genies, both of whom were carrying knives. As Sumaworo watched, these genies circled the area and took their seats. Then Jinna Maghan brought out two more genies who also circled the area and took their seats. After that, the genie chief brought out yet two more who circled and sat down. The number of young male genies was now complete at six.

After those six were arranged, the genie chief reentered the cave and brought out the *bala*,[87] set it down, and went back into the cave. He brought out the mallets and the wrist

---

85. Here, the bard is establishing Sumaworo's "credentials," as it were, to enter the spirit world and negotiate with the genies—his encounter with Jinna Magha is presented as an unusual rite of passage.

86. An apparent contradiction, but possibly meant to indicate that Sumaworo had stepped into the spirit world.

87. Also known as *balafon*, the traditional xylophone. This legendary one is still revered as a sacred object known as the Soso Bala.

bells[88] and laid them on the *bala*. (This was the *bala* you hear about, the one they say came from genies in Manden.)

When the mallets and bells were laid on the *bala*, he went back inside and took out the small drum, *dunun mutukuru*,[89] and set it on the *bala*. Then he put three arrows on the *bala*. Sumaworo wanted those three arrows, so he jumped down from the tree when he saw them laid on the *bala*.

While Sumaworo crouched over the arrows, Jinna Maghan sat down facing the *bala*.

Sumaworo said, "Aah, genie! It was you who led me here. You must have brought me here to see these instruments. If this is true, won't you sell me this *bala*? Please sell me your *bala*. I am the one who made the musical instruments. I made the *kèrèlèngkèngbèng*, I made the *koworo*, I made the *donso nkoni*, the three-stringed *bolon*, the *soron*, and after that I made the *kòra*. But I have never seen this kind of instrument. Please agree to sell this to me. Let me add it to my collection so I can have all the instruments."

What he really wanted, though, were the arrows. His father had moved him out of Folonengbe just for the purpose of acquiring these arrows, for the diviners had said, "These arrows can only be acquired in a foreign land. You cannot acquire them while you are in Folonengbe." (This is why the Mande people have mixed feelings about Sumaworo.)

Jinna Maghan said, "Aha! Sumaworo, you do not have the price of the *bala*."

"Ah," said Sumaworo, "please agree to sell it to me."

"Ah! You say you want to buy this *bala*. But what do you people have that would equal the price of this *bala*?"

---

88. A wooden mallet is held in each hand to strike the melodious, resonating slats of the *bala*, while small brass bells attached to the player's wrist add accompanying rhythm.

89. *Dunun*: a double-headed, cylinder-shaped drum with a name that corresponds to the sound it makes (see n. 75). In Maninka legend, the names of certain instruments become proper nouns, as in the case of Dunun Mutukuru, which, like the sacred *bala* called Soso Bala, is a musical and spiritual icon.

"Sell it to me in *gbensen*." (People of early times used *gbensen*. They would forge a piece of black iron, and cross it the way a Catholic thing[90] looks. This is what we made into our *gbensen*, our money.)

"We do not want *gbensen*. Genies have no use for *gbensen*."

"M'ba, sell it to me for gold."

"Human beings don't have that much gold. God gave gold to the genies."

[In an omitted passage, Jinna Maghan tells a story of Adam asking God for wealth with which to try to return to paradise, and being told that the gold had already been given to the genies and that humans could only reach paradise by avoiding sin, respecting one another, and being faithful.]

Jinna Maghan said, "What do you have to offer us other than gold, cowries, and *gbensen*, which we genies already have?"

Disappointed, Sumaworo said, "Jinna Maghan, I have not met any other genies. You are the only one I have met. If you should decide to sell the *bala*, if you should decide to sell the things that go with it, what would you wish to sell it for?"

Jinna Maghan said, "I am not the only owner of the *bala*. It belongs to all the genies. But the genies say that if they should decide to sell the *bala*, they will only sell it for a human being. All of these instruments together will cost four people. For just the *bala*, one person! One person for the mallets and wrist bells! One person for the small drum! The three arrows that are on it, one person! We will give these things to whoever brings us four people."

Sumaworo was hopeful; he thought he could just capture some ordinary people and give them to the genies. But then Jinna Maghan said, "Sumaworo, we are not talking about just any people, they must all be members of your family. We will

90. Indicating that the *gbensen*, a unit of trade currency made of thick strands of iron wire, was bent into the shape of a rough cross.

give these things to the man who brings us his mother, father, first wife, and sister."

Uh! Sumaworo was disappointed. The genies would not accept any people not related to him.

[In an omitted passage, the narrator informs his listeners that the young hunter Sumaworo had been missing from his homeland for three months, and that he was being searched for by the people of Soso, Manden, Dò ni Kiri, Negeboriya, Tabon, and Kirina, because they did not know that he was in Folonengbe, which was not part of the "seven lands" of Manden.]

Then Sumaworo said to Jinna Maghan, "Tell me to bring ordinary people. I, Sumaworo, am the son of three Touré women,[91] but they are all dead. If they and my father were alive, they would give themselves up to you; then you would have four people. But my mothers and father are dead, I have not married yet, and I have only one sister. My father gave my sister in marriage to the Koroma family in Negeboriya. I would not have agreed to give her up for anything, especially since she is married and has given birth to a boy child. You should agree to let me bring you ordinary people, not relatives."

"Ahuh!" the genie said. "Humans might accept such a deal, but we won't. Forget about these things and go on home. We'll give these things to whomever brings their four relatives to us; no one will get these things without their four relatives."

Sumaworo appealed to them, but finally realized that the genies would not accept his proposal. So he said, "Jinna Maghan, let me take my leave to return to Soso."

Jinna Maghan said, "Go with my blessing."

Sumaworo took his leave and returned to Soso after having lived in the bush for three months. The people in Soso—and

91. According to the tradition, Sumaworo's father was married to three sisters of the Touré family, all of whom are said to be mothers of the Soso *mansa*.

all the people of Manden and Dò ni Kiri—had assumed he was dead. His hair had grown long; it hung from the top of his head to below his neck. News of his arrival spread quickly in Soso. "Oooh," said the people, "the son of the three Touré women has returned! Ooh, Kulanjan,[92] the Kulan of the riverbank, has come back!" They sent a message to Kosiya Kanté, Sumaworo's sister in Negeboriya.

Kosiya Kanté was married to Yerelenko and had given birth to Fakoli. When she heard that her brother had returned, she took Fakoli, put him on her back—even though he could talk, he was still carried on his mother's back—and went to tell her husband. She said, "Sumaworo has been found and I am going to Soso," to which he replied, "Go and see him, find out if he is all right."

Then she went and told Ma Tenenba Condé, "Big sister, my brother has been found, and I am going to see him."

Ma Tenenba Condé said, "If I didn't have to cook for your husband while you're away, I would go with you. My own brothers are in Dò ni Kiri, so I think of Sumaworo as my brother, too. Go and see him; I'll go to see him myself when you come back."

Kosiya Kanté set out for Soso, where she found that people were still celebrating Sumaworo's return.

Kosiya Kanté said, "Hey, Sumaworo, where were you?"

He replied, "Only God knows."

"Listen, Sumaworo, there's no cause for alarm if an apprentice hunter gets lost for fifteen days. But not even an apprentice hunter could stay lost for three months! Where were you? Don't you know how hard your disappearance was for me? Sisters need their brothers. Did you fall out of your hammock? Did your gun barrel blow up? Were you attacked by a leopard?"

"I was not attacked by a leopard."

"Well then, what happened?"

"M'ma, Allah!"

---

92. "Tall Kulan"; hunters (in this case Sumaworo) are praised as the pelican (*kulan*), because it is a hunting bird.

Satisfied that Sumaworo was all right, Kosiya Kanté said, "I didn't tell my husband that I would spend the night here. Please let me go back so I can tell everyone that you are well; they have been worried."

Sumaworo said, "Go with my blessing."

Putting his musket on his shoulder, Sumaworo escorted his sister. When they were one kilometer out of the town, he explained the situation to her.

[In an omitted passage, Sumaworo confides in his sister, cautioning secrecy because of his rival step-brothers. He details his experience with the genies in Folonengbe, describing the wonderful bala *and other objects, including the three magic arrows that he knows he must possess in order to achieve his political ambitions. He tells Kosiya that the genies are demanding a family member in exchange for the* bala, *and he says he will return to renew his pleas that they accept some other human instead.]*

KOSIYA KANTÉ'S SACRIFICE

Kosiya Kanté set off to return to Negeboriya. When she reached the town, she gave Yerelenko and Ma Tenenba Condé the news. Then she sat and thought for a long time. Finally, in the afternoon, she asked Ma Tenenba Condé, "Big sister Tenenba Condé, what would happen to Fakoli if he were to suddenly become an orphan?"

Ma Tenenba Condé said, "What? Little sister Kosiya Kanté, why are you talking like that?"

"Ah, does he usually cry when I leave to look for firewood?"

Ma Tenenba Condé, who was slow to understand, said, "If he's full of porridge when you go to gather firewood, he goes for a long time without crying. He might be mischevious, but he doesn't cry. And thank goodness, for he never stops crying once he gets started."

Once Kosiya heard this about Fakoli being happy when he was filled with porridge, she felt it was possible to leave him. Going into the house, she pounded some soft, clean white rice and put it into a container. The next morning she cooked and cooled a ladle full of the pounded rice. Taking Fakoli into her lap, she fed him the porridge. Then, when he was full of porridge, she gave him her breast. After he suckled it, she gave him the other one, and after he'd suckled that one, he was full.

She took Fakoli to Ma Tenenba Condé and said, "Big sister, take care of Fakoli. I am going to look for firewood."

Ma Tenenba Condé said, "Wait, little sister Kosiya Kanté! I'm worried about the things you said to me yesterday. I'll watch Fakoli while you go to fetch wood, but don't be gone long."

"Uh uh, I won't be long."

So Ma Tenenba Condé took Fakoli and stood him beside her. Going inside, Kosiya Kanté took the wood-chopping axe, the wood-carrying head pad,[93] and the wood-carrying frame; then she went out to the other side of the yard. She looked back at Fakoli, gazing at him for a long time.

On her way out of the yard she again looked back at Fakoli and watched him for a long time. When she arrived at her husband's door, she looked and looked back at Fakoli again; then she entered the house.

From there she left the town and headed into the bush. When she was one kilometer out of town, she heard that Sumaworo had again disappeared, and immediately knew where he had gone. She cut off the beads she wore on her ankles and around her neck. She put the wood-carrying pad

---

93. A doughnut-shaped pad of cloth or twisted grass used to cushion and help balance loads carried on the head.

on her head, tied the carrying frame and axe on top with rope, and ran toward Folonengbe.

[In an omitted passage, Sumaworo continues his negotiations for the bala *and other objects, begging Jinna Maghan to accept any form of payment other than members of his own family.]*

Sumaworo was pleading with Jinna Maghan when Kosiya Kanté arrived. Though Sumaworo had not yet seen her, Jinna Maghan was watching her as she approached. Kosiya Kanté arrived just as Sumaworo was saying, "I will not give away the only sister I have, especially since she is married." Appearing at his side, Kosiya Kanté said, "Sumaworo? It's not up to you to give me away or not. I've come to give myself away. I prefer your success to my life." Then she entered the cave, leaving Sumaworo in tears—the only time in his entire life he ever wept.

Jinna Maghan then said, "Sumaworo, I understand why you are weeping: the genies will never release your sister, and you'll never see her again. But take heart. Remember that we'd agreed on the price of four persons for the *bala* and everything that goes with it? Well, we'll give you the *bala* and everything that goes with it since your sister has given herself to us and we know her sacrifice has touched you deeply. Go on back home and we'll send you the *bala*."

Sumaworo returned home without saying a word to anyone about what had happened. He was deeply troubled, for he and Kosiya Kanté were the only two children of the three Touré women; his only sister was gone. His nephew had been left an orphan. He kept silent and was ashamed to face his in-laws at Negeboriya. The people of Negeboriya were still weeping for Kosiya Kanté on the day Sumaworo finally received the *bala*. Ma Tenenba Condé cried, "Ah! Little sister Kosiya Kanté, is this how you treat me? You leave Fakoli, your own baby, with me, a barren woman? Ah! Kosiya Kanté! Ah! This Kanté woman has real courage!" So cried Ma Tenenba Condé as she went home and reported to her husband.

Yerelenko said, "Tenenba Condé, you should not feel so badly about this. God does as He pleases. I never wanted to marry another woman; it was you who told me to marry again so I could sire my only son. Well, that child was born, and now Kosiya Kanté is gone. Isn't this what you requested from God? That baby is now your son. So do not weep."

That is how God brought an end to Kosiya Kanté.

[In an omitted passage, the narrator advises his listeners on domestic relationships, and how men should comfort their wives when they are in distress.]

TENENBA AND FAKOLI VISIT THE SACRED SITES

Ma Tenenba Condé was calmed by her husband's sweet talk; drying her tears she took Fakoli away to Kani Simbon, the Kulubali ancestor. She said, "Simbon, I have given birth to a child without being pregnant.[94] The Kulubali people and the Condé are very important to each other. You know that if anything bad should happen to Fakoli, the people in both towns will say that Kosiya Kanté meant for it to happen because she abandoned him. They will say, 'A good mother would never give her baby to this woman[95] who has never had a child of her own. Kosiya Kanté must have wanted Fakoli to

---

94. She has become Fakoli's foster mother.
95. Ma Tenenba Condé.

die.'[96] That's what people will say if the Kulubali and Condé
mean anything to each other. So I have brought Fakoli to
you: raise him to be a hunter who will kill game for himself."

They prepared Fakoli, bathing him in protective medicine. The medicines they gave him would prevent him from
dying by fire or defeat at the hands of another man. God
made Fakoli a hunter who could kill animals for himself.

(So it was thanks to a Condé woman that Fakoli was raised
to be a man; it was thanks to a Condé woman that Fakoli
received his *dalilu*.)

Then Tenenba carried Fakoli to Tabon Wana Faran
Kamara at Sibi Mountain and said the same things to him.
She said, "I have brought Fakoli to you so you can set him on
the lap of Jinna Maghan. When you do, you must address the
genie as 'Nya Maghan and Jinna Maghan.'"

Kamanjan carried Fakoli through the entrance of Sibi
Mountain[97] and out through the exit of Tabon Mountain.
Handing Fakoli back to Tenenba Condé, Kamanjan said,
"He has become a hunter who will kill wild game for himself.
Nothing can harm this child now."

From there, Tenenba took Fakoli to Kirina, where she gave
him to Tenen Mansa Konkon. Tenen Mansa Konkon, that
veteran warrior, carried Fakoli into the cave, rolled him in
the dust pit of Kirina, and returned him to Tenenba Condé.

Tenenba then carried Fakoli to Nema and gave him to
Nema Faran Tunkara in Kuntunya.

Returning from Kuntunya, Ma Tenenba Condé took Fakoli
to her brothers in Dò ni Kiri.

Ancestor Donsamogo Diarra said, "Tenenba Condé, you
are the sister who always obeyed me. You were not like Dò
Kamissa. Ha! Have you seen the place where Dò Kamissa settled after she started changing into a buffalo?

---

96. Teneba is saying that if Fakoli dies for any reason she will be blamed
for it; this is why she is taking him on *dalimasigi*, a journey to the sacred
sites of Manden to acquire protective medicines and amulets (*basiw*).

97. This and the reference to an exit refer to a large, natural stone arch
on Tabon Mountain above the village of Sibi, visible from the road running north to Bamako, Mali's capital.

"Ever since you were given in marriage to the people of Negeboriya, you have never returned for a visit. You have never violated our taboo.[98] We have never heard about anything bad happening between you and your husband. Now, if you'd had your own child, you would have spent three months here so we could help you take care of him. So send a message to your husband and ask him to let you spend three months here, so we can prepare Fakoli." (This is why the Koroma[99] *kamalenw* call us Condé "uncles," even though that Condé woman did not give birth to any Koroma.)

Ma Tenenba Condé sent the message to her husband in Negeboriya. Yerelenko replied that she could even stay with the Condé for seven months, just so long as Fakoli became a hunter by the end of her stay.

Our ancestor said, "Ahhh, three months is enough for that." Then he began to prepare Fakoli. To a hat he attached: three hundred and thirteen heads of the kolon bird;[100] the heads of three hundred and thirteen cats; and the heads of three hundred and thirteen *gwara* snakes.[101] When he was done he said, "This hat is for Fakoli." (Whenever Fakoli would put this hat on his head, he would be called "Jamujan Koli." When he wore it he became taller—even when sitting down!—than people who were usually taller than him.[102] This hat came from Dò ni Kiri, and it was the Condé who gave it to him.)

---

98. See n. 35.

99. One of the patronymics or lineage identities (*jamuw*) identified with Fakoli.

100. Not definitively identified, but the skull of the hornbill is favored for sorcerors' bonnets. The numbers of such amulets are purposely exaggerated for emphasis.

101. Very deadly, according to Maninka informants; probably a species of viper, but not positively identified.

102. Reference to the later episode where Fakoli demonstrates his sorcery by increasing his size. "Jamujan" in the praise-name translates as "lengthy *jamu*," possibly referring to Fakoli's many praise-names, or the fact that many blacksmith families claim him as an ancestor.

Donsamogo Diarra said, "But this is not all that I will give to Fakoli." He took the child into a little room and bathed him with water from seven pots. Then, saying, "I will not stop there," Donsamogo Diarra took a horn from the skull of Dò Kamissa's buffalo wraith and prepared it. (The skull of Dò Kamissa's buffalo wraith was our war totem.) After that, he circled Fakoli with the buffalo skull. Then he sat Fakoli on the buffalo skull and said, "This child will not die in fire, he will not die in water; this one has become the nephew of the Condé."

Donsamogo Diarra gathered all of the virgin girls together in a house, in the darkness of the twenty-eighth day of the moon, and put out the lamp. He sent some cotton and spindles in to the girls, telling them to spin the cotton and give it to him in the morning. The girls spun the cotton in the house and in the morning had nine spindles full of thread, which they gave to our ancestor. He took the spindles into his little room, came back out, and gave them to Tenenba Condé, saying, "Go give this thread to the weavers. Let them weave it; let them dip it into the dye. This will be for Fakoli."

The weavers wove the thread; they dipped it into the dye and gave it to Ma Tenenba Condé, saying, "Tenenba Condé, this is for Fakoli."

The cloth was given to Fakoli, who stared at it. "Uh, am I supposed to wear this?" he said. There was not enough cloth to make a hat or a shirt; there was not even enough for a pair of trousers. "Men don't usually wear head-ties. But since my uncles have given me this cloth to wear, I will tie it on my head and wear it as a warrior's headband when I pursue my enemies." (Fakoli's battle headband from Dò ni Kiri is still in Norasoba.)[103]

Finally Ma Tenenba Condé took Fakoli home, where he grew up being grateful to her. Fakoli and Ma'an Sunjata grew up at the same time, and Ma Tenenba Condé had taken Fakoli to all of the same important places visited by Ma'an Sunjata

---

103. A town in Guinea, located on the north bank of the Niger River between Siguiri and Kouroussa.

in his own travels. Fakoli eventually joined the government of Ma'an Sunjata and took part in Sunjata's war with Soso.

[In an omitted passage, the scene shifts back to Soso at the time of Sogolon's visit with her children, when Sumaworo is in power. Sumaworo interprets the meaning of the songs sung earlier by Sogolon. Sunjata violates Sumaworo's sacred taboo, the two men engage in the deadly snuff-taking ritual, and Sunjata is banished from Soso. Continuing the journey into exile, Sunjata violates sacred taboos in each of the places they stop, including Nema, where they remain.]

SUMAWORO'S TYRANNY OVER MANDEN

When Sogolon and her children were staying with ancestor Faran Tunkara at Kuntunya in Nema, he sometimes sent Sunjata on journeys out between the edges of the village and the place where the sun sets. Whenever war broke out, the village sent for Sunjata, who would come and join the Kuntunya army, marching along with them. Whenever he captured three prisoners, he kept one for himself. Whenever he captured five prisoners, he kept two. Whenever he captured ten prisoners, he kept four as his share. (The other six captives were given to the Kuntunya *mansa*.) This is how Sunjata collected his own band of men.

Sunjata stayed in Kuntunya for twenty-seven years, and before the end of the twenty-seventh year, well, things turned very bad in Manden. Things were terrible in Manden!

Sumaworo, who was looking for Sunjata, had sent his warriors to Manden. Whenever Sumaworo consulted Nènèba, his oracle, it would say, "Your successor has grown."

Before consulting Nènèba, Sumaworo first had to have three age sets of young men pile wood beneath Nènèba's cauldron; this had to be done morning and evening, for the oracle always said, "Fire, fire, fire, fire, fire, fire." Then Sumaworo would bathe in the cauldron's medicines whenever he went to visit Nènèba. And Nènèba would tell Sumaworo what to sacrifice before setting out to war.

Every morning Nènèba told Sumaworo, "Sumaworo, only God knows the day. Your successor has grown up."

Sumaworo asked the Mande people, "Has Ma'an Sunjata returned to Manden?" Meanwhile, he laid waste to Manden nine times. The Mande people struggled and rebuilt their villages nine times during Sumaworo's failed search for Sunjata.

Whenever Sumaworo killed some Mande villagers, he would tell his men to search among the bodies for the Condé woman's son. But his men never found Sunjata; instead, they would return saying, "The Mande people do not know the whereabouts of the Condé woman's son."

Sumaworo then summoned all of the Mande villagers to Kukuba. He killed all of the men who attended this meeting except for the leaders Turama'an and Kankejan, who could disappear in broad daylight, and Fakoli, who could stand and vanish instantly. The people who had that kind of *dalilu* were the only ones he did not kill; he killed all of the other men. The people of Manden mourned and wept. But Ma'an Sunjata and his brothers were not there.

After another month had passed, Sumaworo summoned his men to Bantamba, saying, "I have to finish off the Mande. If I do that, I'll find my successor. If I kill all the human beings, my successor will be among them."

So he called the Mande to a meeting in Bantamba. After looking them over he said to his men, "Kill them all." Only those who had the power to disappear in broad daylight escaped. Again Manden wept.

He summoned the Mande to Nyèmi-Nyèmi, and they wept there, too.

Every time Mande people were summoned by Sumaworo, it ended in mourning. Sumaworo was killing the people of Manden, searching among the bodies for his successor. After every massacre, he would go to his Nènèba. (The Kantés now have that Nènèba in Balandugu, the only town they established. Sumaworo's descendants did not establish any other towns, because he was so ruthless.) The Nènèba would say, "Sumaworo, uh heh. You still haven't found him yet? You've killed so many, yet the one you want is not among them."

Sumaworo asked, "What should I do?" To which the oracle replied, "Keep searching for him. He has reached maturity."

When the Mande people were summoned again, this time to Kambasiga, Fakoli went to see Kani Simbon, the Kulubali ancestor.

He said, "Simbon. Manden is about to be wiped out. We must sit down together and find a solution to this problem in Manden. Manden will be reduced to being Soso's peanut farm, because Sumaworo has said two things. He has said, 'Manden's reputation is better than Manden itself,' and 'The Mande women are better than the Mande men.' By this he meant that Manden has only women because he's killed all the men. He said these things to provoke Sunjata, who he now knows to be his successor, into responding." Having said that, Fakoli then returned to Manden and said, "Let us build a council hall at the edge of town, and let the surviving men of Manden hold meetings there. If we don't get together, Manden is doomed." So the men worked hard and built a council hall. Afterwards, they sat in front of the council hall while Fakoli addressed them.

He said, "We have finished building this council hall, which belongs to all of us—except for the one who wants to destroy Manden. If you are a man of courage, this is your council hall. If you are a man of truth, this is your council hall. If you are a master of sorcery, this is your council hall. If you have love for Manden in your heart, this is your council hall."

THE EXPEDITION TO FIND
SUNJATA AND RETURN
HIM TO MANDEN

*[In an omitted passage, the assembled elders decide to summon
diviners to learn who will be the liberator of Manden, and where
he can be found. After an extended period of divination it is
determined that Ma'an Sunjata is the one who was foreseen, and
that a special delegation must be sent to find Sogolon and her
children. Volunteering for this delegation are the Muslim diviners
Manjan Bereté and Siriman Kanda Touré, as well as the female
bard Tunku Manyan Diawara and the female slave Jonmusoni
Manyan. They plan to visit distant markets with special sauce
ingredients that can only be found in Manden, as a way of finding the people they seek.]*

Manjan Bereté laid down his prayer skin[104] as soon as he'd
left town, and made two invocations to God: he asked that
no one would see the travelers leave, and that they would
meet no one on the road. He said, "Siriman Kanda Touré, we
mustn't be seen on the road. It doesn't matter whether you
are a man or a woman: every one of us must use their *dalilu*."
When he'd finished making his two invocations, Manjan
Bereté shook hands with his companions, who asked where
they would sleep that night.

"Ahhh," said Manjan Bereté, "let us try to reach Soso today.
Because tomorrow is Soso's market day."

As a result of his two invocations, each of his companions became invisible when Manjan Bereté shook their
hands. When he gave his hand to one of his companions

---

104. His Muslim prayer rug, the hide of a goat or sheep.

and withdrew it, the person became invisible. Then Manjan Bereté circled his prayer skin and became invisible himself.

They traveled on to the outskirts of Soso, where they spent the night. At daybreak Manjan Bereté said, "Take the things to the market." They set their goods out in the Soso market, but nobody wanted them. They went on to the market of Tabon; but no one wanted what they had. They went to the market of Kirina; no one was interested.

On Thursday they took the road to Kuntunya and slept outside that town to be ready for the market on Friday.

Meanwhile, at a house in that same town, Ma Sogolon Condé was saying to her daughter, "Ma Kolonkan, *aaaoy*! My stomach is hurting me because it's been twenty-seven years since I last had *dado*[105] in Manden. Tomorrow morning, do not wash the dishes, do not scrub the pots; instead, be the first one into the market, my child, and get me some *dado* to eat." (When a *dado* eater goes for a long time without having any, their stomach hurts; this is why Ma Sogolon Condé was complaining all night to Ma Kolonkan. It was a good thing that the Mande people spending the night outside of town had brought *dado*!)

As soon as the sun started to show its face the next morning, Manjan Bereté said, "Take the things into the market." The two women went and sat outside the covered part of the market. They had the *dado* there, along with some *namugu* and some *nèrè* seeds[106] they had on display.

Ma So'olon Wulen Condé said to Ma Kolonkan, "Go early to the market so you can get the *dado* I want." As soon as she'd arrived at the market, Kolonkan saw two women standing there with *dado*. She clapped her hands, saying, "From the time we came from Manden, my mother has not said anything about *dado*, nothing at all. It was only yesterday

---

105. Dried hibiscus blossoms and/or leaves, used as a condiment in sauces.

106. *Namugu* is powdered leaves of the baobab tree, used as an ingredient in sauces. *Nèrè*: *Parkia biglobosa*; the seeds are pounded into a paste that is fermented and rolled into balls to make a pungent condiment called *sumbala*.

that she suddenly spoke of *dado*—and here it is! Heh! My mother has *dalilu.*" She did not even stop to greet the *dado* seller; she immediately reached for the *dado* and put some in her mouth.

Jelimusoni Tunku Manyan Diawara said, "Eh! You, girl, are impolite! Don't touch our merchandise without greeting us or asking us first."

"Eeeh, I was so surprised! My mother told me to come to the market today to see if I could find *dado*. She said she's gone for so long without eating the old things of Manden that her stomach hurts. We haven't seen *dado* since we arrived here; we haven't even seen anyone who sells it. I just wanted to taste it because it is something we always used to have."

Tunku Manyan Diawara asked, "Who are you? Where do you come from?"

"Ah, mother, we come from Manden."

"Who is with you here?"

"I am here with my mother Sogolon Wulen Condé, my elder brother Ma'an Sunjata, and my elder brother So'olon Jamori."

"Aaah! You are the people we have come for! Our road has been good. Let us go to your house."

[In an omitted passage, Kolonkan conducts the Mande delegation to her house for a joyful reunion with Sogolon. Manjan Bereté announces that they have been sent to ask Sogolon to return to Manden because her children are needed there. Sogolon explains that her sons are hunting in the bush and concerns herself with providing the customary hospitality to the guests.]

KOLONKAN FINDS MEAT FOR GUESTS FROM MANDEN

When they had made the visitors from Manden comfortable, Sogolon called, "Ma Kolonkan, come here." When Ma Kolonkan arrived, Sogolon said, "Go and look on the meat-drying rack to see if there's any meat. These Mande people are hungry."

Ma Kolonkan went and looked. She came back and said, "Mother! There's no fresh meat."

"Eh," said Sogolon. "It will take a long time for the dried meat to cook."

Ma Kolonkan told her mother, "just let things be for now." She was happy because she knew that the visitors from Manden would not leave her behind. She had long since reached the age of marriage, and knew she'd be married when she returned to Manden.

Ma Kolonkan went out of the town. She sniffed over here, but did not smell her brothers in that direction. She sniffed over there, but did not smell her brothers in that direction either. When she sniffed in the direction of the sunset, though, she smelled her brothers. She dipped into her *dalilu—shuwe!*—and went after her brothers. Along the way she discovered that they had killed a bushbuck that day. They had also killed a roan antelope. Opening the animals without making any exterior cuts on the carcasses, she removed some internal pieces and took them home. On her return home, she said, "Mother! I went after my brothers, and I have brought back some fresh meat."

Her mother said, "Did you see your brothers?"

"No, but I saw the work they did."

"Did you not tell them that they should meet you in town?"

"I thought you only wanted fresh meat."

"Go and cut the meat into pieces, cook some and put it over rice, and serve it to our guests." So that's what Ma Kolonkan did.

After saying that, Ma So'olon Wulen Condé herself went out of the town in order to signal Ma'an Sunjata. Ma'an Sunjata heard her and said to his younger siblings, "Let's butcher the game; my mother has called me. It's time to go home."

When the brothers went to butcher the roan antelope, they found that its internal organs were missing. And when they went to butcher the bushbuck, they found that its internal organs were missing as well. Ma'an Sunjata said, "Manden Bori, can God create an animal without internal organs?"

Manden Bori said, "Brother, that's not possible. All animals created by God have internal organs. We'll just have to butcher what remains of the animals.

"This was done by our little sister, Ma Kolonkan. Eh! Ma Kolonkan came from town and took out the internal organs of the animals we killed without making any external cuts. Does she have to prove her female powers to us? I won't spare her when I see her in town; she'll soon know that I wear the pants in this family."

(Everyone has his own *dalilu*. That is why it is good for children of the same mother to be in harmony.)

MANDEN BORI'S ANGER
AND KOLONKAN'S CURSE

When the hunters returned, Manden Bori gave Ma Kolonkan the kind of look that is hard to forget. Ma Kolonkan ducked behind her mother.

Manden Bori, who was ready to pounce on his sister, paid no attention to the strangers in the house. Standing his musket against the wall, he pushed his way through the gathering of people. He started to run after Ma Kolonkan, and chased her into the main house. But they did not stop there: they ran into a cooking hut. They ran and ran, and on their way back to the house Manden Bori tripped Ma Kolonkan and threw her down. Her wrapper came loose.

Ma Sogolon Condé said, "Eh! Manden Bori, you are jealous of your sister's *dalilu*."

Ma Kolonkan stood up, saying, "You've shamed me in front of the Mande people. Shamed me! Couldn't you forgive me when I was acting in your own interest?"

Manden Bori touched the fried meat, and the power of his sorcery caused fresh blood to flow from it.

Ma Kolonkan said, "Are you still trying to embarrass me? I was protecting your reputation. The Mande people came to you with the question of kingship. The kingship will eventually be passed to your descendants. But because of what you have done to me today, they will never be able to agree on a ruler until the final trumpet is blown."

[In omitted passages, Tassey Condé digresses to explain how Kolonkan's curse still affects the descendants of Manden Bori in today's Hamana region of Guinea, and what sacrifices would be required to remove the curse. Tassey mentions a childhood experience with his famous father Babu Condé toward the end of the colonial era, and describes how he, Tassey, became the spokesman for the bards of Fadama. Reverting to his story, Tassey describes Sogolon's great happiness at the prospect of her sons returning to Manden. The next episode describes a momentous family meeting of Sogolon and her children, in which the rarely mentioned brother Jamori plays a conspicuous part.]

SOGOLON BESTOWS THE LEGACY OF MAGHAN KONFARA

Sogolon said to her children, "Let us go outside the town. I want to give you my final words." They left the Mande delegation behind and went out of town. When they arrived there, Ma So'olon Condé said to Manden Bori, "Break off that termite mound."[107]

When Manden Bori broke off the termite mound, Sogolon said, "Pick some leaves." He picked some leaves.

She said, "Lay them on the termite mound."

When they were laid on it, she said, "Ma'an Sunjata, you sit on that."[108]

Then she said, "Go and break off another termite mound." So Manden Bori went and broke another one and put leaves[109] on it.

She said, "So'olon Jamori, you sit on that. Now go and break off another one for you to sit on." Manden Bori broke off another termite mound and brought it over.

The three men sat, but Ma So'olon Condé stood up. Ma Kolonkan stood behind her. Women would usually be seated during a hunter's ceremony,[110] but here they did not sit down.

---

107. As the youngest of three sons, Manden Bori is ordered to perform the menial tasks.

108. Of the many kinds of termite mounds (some well over six feet tall), the type referred to here is approximately one to two feet high, shaped like a hard clay mushroom, and the larger ones could be used as stools.

109. For a soft and clean seat.

110. If present at a hunters' meeting, women would be seated in the background. In this and the following line, the bard explains that mother and daughter remain standing because Sogolon is in charge of this solemn occasion.

While they were standing, Ma So'olon Wulen Condé said, "Manden Bori! What I say to you is also for So'olon Jamori and for Ma'an Sunjata[111] to hear. The people of Manden have come for you; they are calling you to war.

"When your father died, Dankaran Tuman wanted your father's gold and silver; he also wanted your father's *dalilu* but did not know where to find it. That's why he has plotted against you all this time: he thought that when he killed you, he could take your father's legacy, his *dalilu*.

"But my sons, you do not have your father's *dalilu*; Dankaran Tuman does not have it either. I have your father's *dalilu* here. If you are seeing that a man's *dalilu* went to his last wife,[112] it is because my husband trusted me. When my husband was dying, he gave his *dalilu* to me so that I could keep it safe and give it to you when you reached maturity. I have brought you here now to give you your father's *dalilu*, because the Mande people have come to take you to war. But what worries me is that there are three things in your father's *dalilu*, and they cannot be separated. They can only go to one person. Ah! There are three things, but your father had three sons. These three things would not be of any benefit to you if we were to divide them up amongst you.

"The Mande messengers have come for your brother Ma'an Sunjata. You must allow him to be given the three things, because the three things—the sorcery horse, the sorcery bow, and the sorcery mask—all work together: when you sit on the sorcery horse, you must also wear the sorcery mask and take up the sorcery bow. Then you are ready for combat against all comers.

---

111. On occasions where oral communication must be precise, it is customary for an important speaker's words to be repeated several times by various people in the presence of the person addressed. When a *jeli* is available, the speaker addresses the bard, who repeats and validates what was just heard. At Sogolon's secret meeting, the youngest son serves to repeat and reaffirm her words (cf. Fakoli's remarks to Sunjata via Turama'an, p. 101, and to Sumaworo via Bala Fasali, p. 105).

112. The legacy would normally go to the first (senior) wife.

"If you mount the sorcery horse without carrying the sorcery bow, or without wearing the sorcery mask, then somebody will strike you down while the horse is galloping. If you put on the sorcery mask without carrying the sorcery bow and you are not on the horse, you will not be able to kill the enemies you see. If you take up the sorcery bow without wearing the mask and without being on the horse, what good is that? The three things must go to one person: please, allow me to give them to Ma'an Sunjata."

So'olon Jamori said, "Manden Bori, tell our mother that I do not agree to what she is saying. Ah! She herself says there are three things. There are three of us. They are easily divided.

"Have you not heard the Mande saying that if you cannot take your father's legacy on your head, you must at least drag part of it behind you? If I cannot carry it, I will drag it behind me. Let her bring the three things out and divide them between the three of us."

Ma So'olon Condé said, "Eh, So'olon Jamori my son! Eh, So'olon Jamori! I was afraid you'd cause trouble; that is why I wanted to bring you out of the town. Did you not hear me say that there are three things, but they can only solve one problem? Will you not be agreeable?"

Manden Bori said, "Big brother So'olon Jamori,[113] will you not have pity on our mother, who is so worried about this? Let us agree to give the *dalilu* to brother So'olon Maghan."

Ah! Jamori said if Manden Bori did not shut his mouth, he would slap his ears.

Manden Bori said, "You can't slap my ears. Why should you slap my ears for this? Don't you know our brother can battle Soso with or without our father's legacy?

"And who used up our mother's legacy? You and I did; our brother did not take part in that. Our mother took her gold earring and silver bracelet and gave them to Sansamba

---

113. In many variants of the epic, Sogolon's son Jamori is not mentioned at all, and the claim here that Manden Bori was the youngest of the three brothers is an especially rare detail.

Sagado, the Somono ancestor, as a future day's river-crossing fee.[114] And how many of us got into the canoe that day, when we left Manden by crossing the river? The canoe our mother paid for with her legacy? Our mother went in the canoe, our little sister got into the canoe, you got into the canoe, and I got into the canoe. Did our brother get in? Hah! Didn't our brother say he was not getting in? Didn't my mother weep? Didn't he say that we should go ahead and he would follow? And by the time we got to the other side of the river, didn't we see our brother already sitting there?

"The *dalilu* with which our brother crossed the river was our father's legacy, and Sunjata can battle Sumaworo with that. But you say you will slap my ears? Why didn't you slap my ears on the riverbank?"

Ma'an Sunjata said, "Manden Bori, be quiet. Tell my mother that we will not quarrel. If you see somebody taking your friend's share of the sauce, your own sauce cannot satisfy you. Does she think I will quarrel with this foolish person? I will never quarrel with So'olon Jamori over our father's legacy. Even if he were to ask me to give it all to him, I would do it. Tell my mother to bring out the legacy.

"But mother, we will never forget the two things you have done for us. First, we were legitimately born, and it is because of our legitimacy that the Mande people came to find us. Second, my father married fifty women—fifty wives!—and two other women, none of whom gave birth to a child. Sansun Bereté was one of the other two women: she gave birth to Dankaran Tuman and Nana Triban.

"But you! You were the fifty-second wife. Eh! Out of all his wives, why did my father give his legacy to you? Because of your devotion, and it was for us you were so devoted. I trust in God. Even if you do not give me the legacy, I will vanquish Sumaworo because of your devotion. Bring out the legacy."

Ma So'olon Wulen Condé said, "I am pleased with that, now excuse me." She pushed her hand into her abdomen.

114. See p. xxii.

When she did that, *ho!* The *dalilu* fell out. When the three *dalilu* were piled together, Ma'an Sunjata laughed.

He started to say, "So'olon Jamori," but suddenly his mother began to shake. So'olon Ma'an held his mother until her dizziness passed. When the dizziness left her eyes, Sunjata said, "Manden Bori, tell our mother that she should tell So'olon Jamori he should choose one of the things. Aheh! My little brother and I will not quarrel over my father's legacy."

So'olon Jamori said that he chose the sorcerer's mask. They asked, "Is that your choice?" And he replied, "Uhuh, that is mine." They said, "Very well, take it."

Sunjata said, "Manden Bori, choose one."

Manden Bori said, "I will not take a share in this legacy. I am holding your shirt-tail, and so long as I hold your shirt-tail, nothing will happen to me in the war with Soso. When you die, Sunjata, your legacy will come to me anyway. It was my father's legacy, but you are my father now, and so it belongs to you. Take both my share and your share."

Ma'an Sunjata said, "Is that your word?"

"Uhuh. It is your name, not mine or So'olon Jamori's, that will become attached to the bow and *mansaya*[115] we are quarreling over." (That is why, when people go outside town for a private meeting, they say, "Let us speak with the truth of Manden Bori.")

Manden Bori, the youngest of the brothers, had his oldest brother's blessing. Ma So'olon Wulen Condé spoke. She said, "Manden Bori, is that your word? Come here."

Taking Manden Bori behind a bush, Sogolon said, "Manden Bori, you've honored me, and so now God will honor you. Nobody will ever dishonor you. If you'd acted the way So'olon Jamori acted, then all of the Mande people would know that your father's *dalilu* had been divided—and if your rival knows your secret, he will vanquish you. You preferred to keep all of this secret so I would not be shamed.

"Come and let me give you my legacy. My legacy is something that did not come from here, in Nema, or Manden. It

---

115. The bow and quiver were symbolic of Mande kingship (*mansaya*).

came from Dò ni Kiri, the home of my brothers. I will give this ring to you. So long as you live, it will protect you from genies or enemies that might threaten you; it will also keep you safe in the bush. If you find yourself in trouble, look at this ring and say, 'Ah, mother!' If you do that, God will protect you. If you look at it and say, 'Ah, genie!' God will save you from genies. If you look at it and say, 'Genie and man!' God will spare you from both." (That was the first of the brass rings hunters now wear on their fingers. Some people call such a ring "genie and man.") Sogolon said, "This is your keepsake." Then they all returned to town.

[In the next scene, Sogolon suddenly dies and Sunjata tells Manden Bori to request a plot of land for her burial.]

THE BURIAL OF SOGOLON AND DEPARTURE FROM NEMA

On the path to town, Manden Bori met with Faran Tunkara, the *mansa* of Nema. He said, "Mansa, my brother says that I should come and tell you that my mother is dead. He'd like you to agree to give him some land he can use for her burial."

Now, Faran Tunkara had been unhappy to see the messengers from Manden arrive in Nema. From the time Sunjata arrived in Nema, he'd helped the Kuntunya people win every single battle they'd faced, and he returned with slaves from every campaign. But Faran Tunkara could not keep Sunjata in Nema, because Sogolon and her family had arrived there by choice. He decided to start a quarrel so he could detain Sunjata.

So Nema Faran Tunkara said, "Manden Bori, go and tell your brother that I, Nema Faran Tunkara, say that I own all the land here. Unless you brought a piece of land with you from Manden to bury your corpse in, you should load her body on your head and carry it back to Manden the same way you brought her. Tell him that if you bury her in my land, I will blast her out of the ground with gunpowder. Go and tell your brother that."

Manden Bori returned on the path and relayed Nema Faran Tunkara's message to Sunjata. When he heard what Manden Bori reported, Manjan Bereté said, "What kind of man is Nema Faran Tunkara? Simbon, let me go and give him a real 'message.'"

"Eee," said Sunjata, "just leave it alone. Don't worry, he'll provide the land. I've spent twenty-seven years here; I'm in his army. And he says I should carry my mother's body back to Manden? He'll soon provide the land."

To Manden Bori, Sunjata said, "Go back and tell Nema Faran Tunkara that I, the son of the Condé woman, say he should give me some land in which I can bury my mother. Tell him it is I who say so."

When Tunkara was told this, he said to Manden Bori, "I do not want ever to see you here again. From the minute you first arrived here, I knew that you're a hotheaded man. Go and tell your brother that I don't go back on what I've said twice. Tell him I have no land for him here."

Manden Bori went and told this to Ma'an Sunjata. Manjan Bereté and Siriman Kanda Touré became angry. They were all brave men; they all had *dalilu*, and they all knew how to fight. But when they started to leave the house to find Nema Faran Tunkara, Ma'an Sunjata said, "Be patient and take your seats. He will soon provide the land."

Sunjata took the path that passed behind the house. Along the way, he picked up a fragment of old clay pot, a piece of old calabash, the feather of a guinea fowl, and a partridge feather. To these things he added a stick of bamboo. He gave all of these things to Manden Bori, and said, "Tell Tunkara that I say he should give me land to bury my mother in. If he's asking a price for his land, well, tell him I'll pay his fees with these things. Tell him he must agree to let me lay my mother in the ground."

As he gave Faran Tunkara these things from Sunjata, Manden Bori said, "My brother says this is payment for your land, and that you should agree to let him bury his mother."

Faran Tunkara said, "Is this what you pay for land in your country? Huh, Manden Bori? I do not ever want to see you here again. Take these things and go away."

But Tunkara's *jeli* man, who was sitting there beside him, said, "He should not take those things away from here. Heh! Sunjata has sent you an important message.

"M'ba, when these people came to Nema, didn't I say you should kill Sunjata? And didn't you reply that Sunjata had come to place himself in your care, and that therefore you must not do anything to him? Ahuh! Well, now he has said something to you; there's a message in these things he sent. Since you do not understand the message, I will tell you what these things mean."

To which Faran Tunkara replied, "All right, tell me what they mean."

The *jeli* said, "This piece of bamboo means that you should give him land so he can bury his mother in it. If you do not give him land, the Mande people will come and take it for themselves. If he should be named king after he finishes fighting that war for Manden, he will bring the Mande army here to Nema, and he will break Nema like this old clay pot or this old calabash. Then the guinea fowls and the partridges will take their dust baths in the ruins of Nema. See? These are the feathers of those guinea fowls and partridges. Nothing will grow in the ruins of Nema but weeds; that's what this piece of bamboo stick means."

Now, Mansa Tunkara was a good debater, and he always won arguments. So he said, "I am right."

The *jeli* said, "How can you be right about this?"

"I am right," said Faran Tunkara, "because these people have been here for twenty-seven years. During the time those three brothers served in my army, I lost no battles. They never cheated me, were never disobedient to me; I never had to discipline them for chasing women. Now their mother has died. Are they going to do the right thing and say the corpse is mine, or are they just going to demand that I give them land?"

Everyone agreed that the three brothers should have observed the custom of saying, "This is your corpse."

Faran Tunkara said, "Ah! This is why I refused. Eh! If they were raised correctly as children, they should have said that God has made this my opportunity, and that this is my corpse. But did they show me the proper respect? Should they be looking for land to lay their mother in?"

Everybody said, "You are right!" Even Manjan Bereté himself came and said, "You are right."

"Very well," said Faran Tunkara. "If I am right, give her to me and I will conduct the funeral."

Even though she was a woman, the people of Nema gave Sogolon a man's funeral. They killed cows, fired their guns, and beat the special drum. (This tradition started with Ma So'olon Wulen Condé's funeral.) Then they took her body to the town of Kuntunya, and on Thursday they buried her.

When they were finished with the burial, Simbon asked for Faran Tunkara's permission to leave Nema. Because all debts had now been settled between the two men, Sunjata was able to say, "I will leave tomorrow."

Faran Tunkara said, "Go with my blessing. I give you the road." But once Sunjata and his brothers had returned to their house, Faran Tunkara summoned his warriors, telling them, "I cannot allow Sunjata to leave with his men, because those men are rightfully mine; Sunjata had no men of his own until he arrived here. Prepare yourselves and go on ahead to cut them off. Go ahead as far as the second village and wait for them there; attack them when they arrive, and try to capture them. If you bring them back, they will never leave Nema again."

Faran Tunkara's warriors left, passing the first village and preparing their attack at the second. And when Sunjata and his companions arrived at the second village, they were attacked. So'olon Jamori did not survive the attack! He died there; he did not live to reach Manden. So the three parts of his father's legacy were combined and given to Simbon. (That is why we say that if a *kamalen* of the Mansaré lineage becomes selfish, do not bother to curse him. He won't live long.)

Sunjata and his men escaped that ambush, and Sunjata added the captives they took from among Faran Tunkara's warriors to his own troops.

[The narrator explains that despite the ambush that killed So'olon Jamori, Faran Tunkara sent troops to support Manden's campaign against Soso, and Sunjata never attacked Nema. Claiming that he wants to notify Sumaworo of his return so he will not be accused of sneaking back into Manden, Sunjata stops in Soso. Sumaworo issues a series of warnings to Sunjata that he must not attack Soso. They engage in a traditional boasting contest, concluding with Sunjata's vow to return and Sumaworo's reply that he will be waiting.]

THE RETURN OF SUNJATA

Sunjata took the road toward home. When they arrived at the edge of town, the townspeople could hear *nege* music[116] played by Jelimusoni Tunku Manyan Diawara.

She sang to Manden:

> "The *danama yirindi*[117] that we have been looking for,
> He is at the edge of town.
> Come, let us go.
> For the sake of the Condé woman's son,
> Come, let us go.
> The person that Manden was busy searching for,
> Known as So'olon Ma'an,
> Come, let us go."

Sansamba Sagado crossed the river with his canoe that day. He put the canoe into the river without a pole or paddle, and as soon as he untied the canoe, it headed straight for Sunjata and his men—*prrrr*, just as if it had a motor.

Sunjata loaded his men into the canoe and said, "You will now see the power of my *dalilu*." He struck the water, the canoe went *prrrr*, and they landed on the riverbank in Manden, where Simbon stepped out. His fathers, brothers, and all the men of Manden were there to greet and embrace him. (The shade tree under which the people of Manden welcomed Sunjata home is still living today.) When he arrived, Manden was jubilant, Manden celebrated. They named that place Nyani, the town of happiness, the town of rejoicing, *ko anyè nyani so.*[118]

---

116. *Nege* = iron; also a synonym for the *nkarinyan*, a rhythm instrument consisting of a notched iron tube seven to eight inches long, held in one hand and scraped with a thin metal rod.

117. Roughly translated as "superhero" (see p. 56 for alternate usage).

118. This and the following line comprise a popular etymology (see n. 37).

As the people of Manden welcomed Sunjata and his men, they said, "Manjan Bereté, you are welcome; Siriman Kanda Touré, you are welcome; Tunku Manyan Diawara, you are welcome; Jonmusoni Manyan, you are welcome.[119] You have brought a gift for Manden: you have found Simbon! We knew that someday the son of Farako Manko Farakonken and the Condé woman would return. But Manden suffered while he was away; we have suffered so much at Sumaworo's hands. Let Sunjata see for himself how many of those he knew here have been killed by Sumaworo. The only people left here are those with *dalilu*, and Sumaworo has even caused those who have *dalilu* to suffer.

"When we knew Sunjata was returning, we carried out divinations and swore oaths and saw that only he could receive ancestor Mamadi Kani's legacy.[120] And now that he has come, heh! We all—the Kulubali, the Konaté, and the Douno—say that he should accept the legacy and help Manden. Simbon, you have been called to take the legacy." (This saying—"Take your legacy," or *ko ila kè ta*—came to be spoken as "Keita.")

CONDÉ PRIDE AND DESCENT FROM ADAMA

[In the following brief departure from his narrative, the bard (who is traditionally expected to instruct as well as entertain) reiterates his view of human origins and explains who really built Paris.]

---

119. The four people listed here are famous for their journey to find Sunjata and bring him back from exile (see p. 80).

120. Passed from ancestor Mamadi Kani (p. 7) to Sunjata's father (p. 87).

These days, when someone talks about the Tontajontaniwooro,[121] they are talking about us: Fadama was part of
that. And that is why, as God is my witness, anybody who
wants to take our *jeliya* from us[122] will not succeed. I'm telling
you, we will not surrender our *jeliya.*

Tontajontaniwooro! No one is older than us, and no one
has ever defeated us. Everyone wanted us to help them fight
their wars, because nobody could defeat us; we possess all the
dalilu of war.

You might hear a Condé *kamalen* claim he has nothing, that
his mother did not give him anything. But I swear to God, a
Condé *kamalen* did get something! The Maninka of the seven
jamanaw are beholden to no one![123] We fought against everyone; nobody defeated us. And that is why we're able to tell
people that, just as the Americans are the best of the white
people, so the Condé are the best among the blacks.

Let me tell you some more about this. We—the Africans
and the Americans, white people and black, all of us—all
descended from the same ancestor, Isiaaka. Don't you know
this? Ancestor Adama sired us all. Adama's first child was
Sita![124] Sita's child was Yunusi! Yunusi's child was Hayayulu!
Hayayulu's child was Fariku! Fariku's child was Iyada! Iyada's

---

121. Lit. "sixteen slaves who carried the quiver," a mnemonic term
referring to the oldest lineages of Manden who are recalled not literally
as "slaves" but as staunch supporters of Sunjata in unifying the ancient
jamanaw into the basis of empire.

122. The following lines are related to the fact that, among the great
numbers of Maninka people named Condé, only those from Fadama
are bards, while the primary occupational identity of people named
Kouyaté and Diabaté is *jeliya,* and the latter are generally recognized as
the earliest *jeli* lineages, although Tassey denies this.

123. *Jeliw* are customarily regarded as dependent on patrons whom they
serve as orators and musicians. Tassey boasts that the Condé bards were
never beholden to anyone, thus implying that their historical discourse
is less influenced by such obligations.

124. See notes 7 and 8. In addition to Adam, a few other names identified as Prophets in the Koran are recognizable in the following lines,
including Seth (Ar. S͟hīt͟h, Tassey's "Sita"), who was the third son of
Adam and Eve, Luqman (Lamaki), and Noah (Nuha).

child was Kanuga! Kanuga's child was Lamaki! Lamaki's child was Nuha, who was carried by the flood when the whole world was destroyed.

When the water receded, Nuha sired three sons: Sama, Hama, Yafisu.[125] Sama sired Shalihu, Shalihu sired Hamidu, Hamidu sired Salimaya, Salimaya sired Hajara. It was Hajara who sired our ancestor Ibrahima.[126] Now hear what we, the *jelilu*, are telling you: it was Ibrahima who built the Kaaba.[127] Ibrahima sired two sons: Ishmaila, and Isiaaka.

Ishmaila! The Nyiminyeme[128] descended from him.

Isiaaka! We, the Condé, descended from him, and that's why we're able to say that no one is better than us. What have we to fear?

All of these modern scientists—the ones who make airplanes fly! make watches! make radios!—they're all Isiaaka's descendants, just like us! One time a Frenchman asked my father if he knew anything about how Paris was built. My father said, "Yes, I know something: the history of Paris. This Paris you ask about, it was not built by Frenchmen! It was not built by Americans! It was not built by the English! It was not built by the Russians! None of them built it. They only saw it appear. And because they only saw it appear, they called it

---

125. In the Koran: Sām, Hām, and Yāfi<u>th</u>; in the Bible: Shem, Ham, and Japheth.

126. According to the *Shorter Encyclopedia of Islam* (1965: 154), the names of Abraham's ancestors extend back through six ancestors to Shāli<u>kh</u> (Tassey's "Shalihu"), and through two more generations to Sām (Shem) and Nū<u>h</u> (Noah).

127. Ar. Ka'ba (lit. "cube"). A large, nearly cubic stone structure covered by a black cloth that stands in the center of the Grand Mosque of Mecca. This and a black stone inside its southeastern corner represent a sanctuary consecrated to God. According to Islamic tradition, God ordered Adam to build the Ka'ba, and Gabriel taught him the pilgrimage ceremonies; it was rebuilt by Adam's son Seth, later rebuilt by Ibrāhīm (Abraham) and his son Ismā'īl (Ishmael), and then rebuilt many times thereafter.

128. One of the many names for the Prophet in Mande tradition. In Islamic belief, Abraham is the ancestor of Muhammad through Abraham's son Ishmael.

'Paris.'" My father said this because if Paris was ever built by anyone, it was God.

Here's what I have to say to you: do not be too concerned with blackness or whiteness; be more concerned with humanity. We are all equal. We all have life. We all go to sleep. We all eat food. We all suckle our mother's breasts. So when you come to visit us, you have come to your father's home.

[In an omitted passage, Sunjata accepts the leadership of Manden, and an elaborate series of sacrifices is performed in preparation for war against Soso.]

FAKOLI REVEALS HIS POWER

While the Mande men were in a meeting, a message from Sumaworo arrived. He said that he'd been waiting a long time for a message from the Mande. He said it had been a long time since their *mansa* arrived, and that he'd not seen any Mande messengers. Finally, Sumaworo said that since So'olon Ma'an had now returned home, he wanted to see all of the Mande people at Dakajalan on the fourteenth of the new month. The battle had now been set.

As soon as he heard Sumaworo's message, So'olon Ma'an replied by having his people beat the signal drum, calling everyone to the council hall. On his way to the council hall, Fakoli was thinking, "We are going to march against Soso!" But his mother and Sumaworo had suckled at the same breast, and he wondered if it was right for him to join the Mande people in attacking Sumaworo. He decided, "As soon as I get to the council hall, I will ask the Mande people to let me go to Soso. Let Manden come and fight both me and my uncle."

But before Fakoli had the chance to say this to the men gathered in the council hall, Manden Bori laughed at him. Manden Bori always ridiculed Fakoli whenever he entered the council hall. When he heard Manden Bori laughing at him, Fakoli became angry and said, "Turama'an, let me give you a message for Simbon. Tell Simbon to ask his younger brother why he always laughs at me. Of all the people that enter the council hall, it's me that Manden Bori laughs at. Why does he laugh at me? What have I done to him?"

When Ma'an Sunjata was given this message, he said, "Manden Bori, stop laughing at Fakoli. Didn't you hear him saying that you are shaming him? Why do you laugh at him?"

Manden Bori replied, "Big brother, the tall men always duck their heads as they enter the council hall. Though Fakoli is only one and a half arm-spans tall, he also ducks his head when he comes in. That is what makes me laugh. Aaah, that Fakoli, heh, heh."

Fakoli said, "Turama'an, tell Simbon that he should tell his younger brother that short Mande people can do things that tall Mande people cannot do. And he'd better believe it"

Manden Bori said, "I won't believe that until I see it. Really, do you believe that? I don't."

Fakoli picked up his goatskin rug and, placing it in the center of the council hall, sat down on it. He waved his hand and grunted. He raised the roof from the house! The sun shone in on everybody. He said, "Well, Manden Bori, what about that?"

Manden Bori said, "You spoke the truth."

(They were fair about crediting one another with the truth, for there was respect among those with *dalilu*.)

The people asked Fakoli to put the roof back where it belonged. They said, "No tall Mande man has ever done such a thing."

Then Fakoli placed his hand in the middle of the council hall floor. He crouched there and wrinkled his face. Wrinkled his face and wrinkled his face! He squeezed everyone against the wall. That was the origin of the song "Nyari Gbasa," which goes:

"Fakoli, our arms will break,
Fakoli, our heads will burst,
Fakoli, our stomachs will rupture."

(That song belongs to the Koroma family.)

The people said, "Fakoli, stop! No tall Mande man has done such a thing."

FAKOLI EXPLAINS HIS DILEMMA AND TAKES HIS LEAVE FROM MANDEN

After performing these feats, Fakoli spoke to the assembled elders. He said, "Turama'an, Simbon, and everyone in the council hall: Sumaworo has sent a message that we should meet at Dakajalan. But my mother and Sumaworo were the children of the three Touré women, and it would be shameful for me to participate in Manden's attack on my uncle. I ask that you give me leave to go to Soso. I should be at my uncle's side when you come to attack him."

Ma'an Sunjata heard what Fakoli said, even though Manden Bori refused to repeat it to him. To Manden Bori, Sunjata said, "Haven't I told you? Fakoli is right. You and I have uncles whose home is Dò ni Kiri. What if we knew that Dò ni Kiri would be attacked? Would we stay here and do nothing?"

Manden Bori said, "Would anyone dare to attack Dò ni Kiri?"

"That's not the point. If Fakoli says he is going to help his mother's kinsman, leave him alone and let him go." Then, turning to Fakoli, Sunjata said, "Fakoli, you have done well by Manden. You helped us during Sumaworo's nine invasions of Manden, and our nine efforts to rebuild our homeland. So if you should say that you are going to help your uncle, very well; we won't stop you. But remember that if we meet on the battlefield there will be no brotherhood, no friendship between us. Don't think us ungrateful. But there's no gratitude when the guns start firing. That is all I have to say."

Fakoli said, "Bisimillahi," and returned to his house for the night.

The next morning Fakoli bathed in the water of his seven medicine pots. Taking his battle-axe on his shoulder, he brought out his horse and mounted it. His groom, Nyana Jukuduma,[129] was with him. He lifted up his wife, Keleya Konkon, and sat her behind him on his horse; then he took the ends of his scarf and tied them together, saying, "Because I know the kind of man my uncle is, he might wait for me on the road."[130]

While he was preparing to leave, another message from Sumaworo arrived. Sumaworo said that he'd been informed of Fakoli's plan to help him fight against Manden, and that Fakoli must not go to Soso. Sumaworo said he'd learned that if the Mande were successful in defeating him, they planned to replace Sumaworo with Fakoli as ruler of Soso. When the people of Soso heard this, they promised to cut off Fakoli's head, just as the Mande people already wanted to. Thus, one way or another, said Sumaworo, Fakoli's "feet would be bringing his head" if he dared to come to Soso. Fakoli laughed, "I'm not going to die for anyone—not Sunjata, and not Sumaworo." (Even today, that expression is often quoted.)

Fakoli said, "Go and tell my uncle that I'll soon be there. If I were really planning to get myself killed, then I'd let him carry out his threats against me. But since I don't intend to die, I'll go to Soso today. Tell him to get ready."

[In an omitted passage, Sumaworo deploys soldiers to intercept Fakoli and kill him, but Fakoli makes himself and his companions invisible and arrives unscathed at the gates of Soso.]

---

129. A slave that cared for his horse.
130. To ambush him.

FAKOLI FINDS
TROUBLE IN SOSO

When Sumaworo learned that Fakoli was accompanied only by his wife and his slave, he told Bala Fasali,[131] "Take the *bala* and welcome my nephew."

Bala Fasali took up the *bala* and sang the song we now call "Janjon":[132]

> "Eh, Fakoli!
> You became a son.
> If death is inevitable,
> A formidable child should be born.
> The Mande people said
> That if you came, they would wait for you on the road.
> The people of Soso said
> That if you came, your feet would bring your head.
> Knowing that, you still had no fear.
> If death is inevitable,
> A formidable child should be born."

Sumaworo welcomed Fakoli by standing and raising his elephant tail in salute. Fakoli sat down and explained why he had come to Soso. He said, "Bala Fasali, you take part in this.[133] Let Sumaworo hear what I have to say. I have come because Sumaworo has done many things, and though I was invisible as I traveled, I come in good faith.

---

131. An unusual pronunciation of this famous bard's name, which is usually given as Bala Fasaké, or a variant thereof.

132. One of the oldest and most famous songs of Manden, said to have been originally composed for Fakoli, but in later times played to honor any distinguished personage.

133. Custom dictated that the dignitary, in this case Fakoli, would speak to the *jeli*, who would then add weight to the message by repeating it to the person addressed (see n. 111).

"The three Touré women gave birth to my mother and to Sumaworo. I have been thinking about my mother ever since war was declared between Soso and Manden. Had my mother been a man, she would have fought in this war alongside Sumaworo, her brother. That is why I decided to come: to fight in place of my mother. I have come to Sumaworo through the will of God; let us unite and fight the coming war together."

Sumaworo replied, "Bala Fasali, I'll tell you what to say to Fakoli. Tell him that I appreciate his words, and that I am pleased he has come."

After this meeting, Fakoli was taken to meet Sumaworo's wives. Sumaworo had three hundred and thirty-three wives. Fakoli had only one wife, Keleya Konkon.

To his three hundred and thirty-three wives, Sumaworo said: "Fakoli has arrived just as I am going to war. The oracle Nènèba says that in order to win this war I must offer three hundred and thirty-three different dishes as sacrifice. I want these dishes to be prepared the day after tomorrow, on Friday. I mention this because Fakoli should know about this sacrifice if we are to be allies."

Fakoli said, "Fine. Since I have come to take the place of my mother, my wife will cook the one bowl of food my mother would have provided."

When the Soso women heard Fakoli say that, they said, "Paki! We'll show that Mande woman how much better a Soso woman's cooking is." This was insulting to Keleya Konkon, who said, "I'm going to build my fire near theirs. Fakoli, go and find a cooking pot for me. Those Soso women want to brag? They'll soon learn that Mande women can also cook. They will realize that Manden has kitchens, too." Fakoli left to find a cooking pot for Keleya Konkon.

Among the three hundred and thirty-three dishes prepared by Sumaworo's wives were beans, rice, fonio, cereal paste, millet wafers, wheat meal, cassava, and porridge: all of these different foods were included in the sacrifice.

Fakoli's wife said to him, "Bring me rice, pounded cassava, and fonio for my pot. God willing, I'm going to cook a meal that the *jelilu* will sing about for years to come."

Keleya Konkon put her one pot on the fire. Whenever she saw the Soso women who were cooking rice put some into their pots, she would put rice in her one pot, then sit down. Whenever she saw the Soso women who were cooking fonio put some into their pots, she would add some fonio in her one pot then sit down.

When the women who were cooking *monie*[134] were rolling their *monie* balls, Keleya Konkon also rolled *monie* balls. When the women put the *monie* balls into their pots, Keleya Konkon would put *monie* balls into her pot too, then take her seat. When the women who were baking *takura*[135] were putting their *takura* balls into their pots, Keleya Konkon also put *takura* balls into her pot, then sat down.

So Keleya Konkon put into her one pot all of the same things the Soso women put into their three hundred and thirty-three pots. Then, when the women started dishing out rice, she took her rice bowl and dished out the rice from her pot. When the women started dishing out the fonio, she took her fonio bowl and dished out her fonio from the same pot.

Sumaworo's wives produced three hundred and thirty-three dishes—but Fakoli's wife also produced three hundred and thirty-three dishes, and all from her one pot! The wives couldn't get the best of her.

Some scandalmongers went to Sumaworo and told him what had happened, adding, "Didn't we tell you that Fakoli came to take your place? You have three hundred and thirty-three wives, who have cooked you three hundred and thirty-three dishes. Your nephew has only one wife, but she has also prepared three hundred and thirty-three dishes! In fact, Keleya Konkon's servings are bigger than yours! Everything that you have, Fakoli now also has. He came to take your

---

134. A millet porridge made with small balls of millet flour flavored with tamarind or lemon.

135. A millet cake made with five balls of soaked millet flour and baked or steamed in a clay pot buried in the ground; one of the preferred foods for sacrifice or alms-giving.

place. If you don't take this Fakoli business seriously, he will take Soso away from you even before you go to war."

Sumaworo said, "Huh? Oho!" And he called his people together. Sumaworo sent the scandalmonger to go and bring Fakoli to the meeting.

Instead of going to find Fakoli, the scandalmonger simply went and stood on the road, then returned to Sumaworo, saying, "I have called him." A lot of time passed; Fakoli did not come to see Sumaworo. When Sumaworo sent for someone, he expected that person to arrive one minute after the messenger returned.

"Ah!" said Sumaworo. "Did you not see my nephew?"

To which the scandalmonger replied, "I saw him."

"Ah, did you not call him?"

"I called him."

"All right, go and tell him I am waiting for him."

The scandalmonger went and stood in the road again. Returning to Sumaworo, he said, "I have called him."

More time passed and still Fakoli did not appear. Now very angry, Sumaworo sent another messenger to get Fakoli. He said, "You go and tell Fakoli that I am waiting for him."

That messenger did find Fakoli. He said, "Fakoli, this is the third time you have been called. Why didn't you come when we called? Who do you think you are?"

Fakoli said, "Me? Was I called three times?"

"Yes, the message came and came again."

"Me? M'ba, I refuse."

That messenger ran back and told Sumaworo, "Your nephew refuses to come."

Sumaworo said, "*Paki*! That's it! Fakoli dares tell me, Sumaworo, 'I refuse'?"

Once Sumaworo's last messenger had gone, Fakoli put on his hat with the three hundred birds' heads. He put his axe on his shoulder and tied his headband around his head, because he knew there was going to be trouble.

When Sumaworo saw Fakoli approaching, he stood up in his royal seat and said, "Fakoli, am I the one to whom you said, 'I refuse'?"

Fakoli replied, "I refuse," for he believed it would be cowardly to explain himself to Sumaworo.

Again, Sumaworo asked, "Am I the one to whom you said, 'I refuse'?"

"I refuse."

"Why?"

"I refuse."

"Ah, very well." Sumaworo said. "What they told me is the truth. You claim that you came to help me. But you have not come to help me. You know what you came for. I have three hundred and thirty-three wives who have prepared three hundred and thirty-three dishes for me. You have only one wife, yet she also produced three hundred and thirty-three dishes for you.

"Did you come to help me? Were you told that your head and my head are equal? I gave you this wife you're so proud of—the one with your mother's name[136]—and now I am taking her back. You can't brag about what you don't have anymore! This Kosiya Kanté that you have, she is my daughter,[137] so now I am taking her back."

Fakoli said, "Ah! Uncle, have matters between us sunk so low? Has our dispute come to the point of taking back a wife? You can have her! I don't even want her now, at least not until the smoke from our battle with the Mande people at Dakajalan has settled. Until then, I don't want her!"

He brought out his blanket and tore off a strip, *prrr!* He threw it to Keleya Konkon and told her to use it for a mourning veil, saying, "I will not marry you again until

---

136. Fakoli's mother was Kosiya, so his wife Keleya was not exactly her namesake.

137. Family relationships among Manding peoples are perceived on several levels, or "paths." Keeping in mind that this is the storyteller's viewpoint, this is probably meant in the sense that the wife Sumaworo provided for Fakoli was a classificatory "daughter" of Sumaworo. In Manding societies, the children of one's cousins are considered to be one's own children.

I've defeated your brother[138] in gunsmoke. I am returning to Manden."

Turning his back on Keleya Konkon, he gave the tail of his horse to Nyana Jukuduma,[139] and the two men took the road to Manden, where the diviners were still praying to God.

When Fakoli got back to Manden, he went and stood at the door of the council hall. He said, "Simbon, my uncle and I have quarreled. He has taken my wife from me. I will not take back Keleya Konkon until I do it in gunsmoke."

"Huh," Ma'an Sunjata laughed.

Manjan Bereté and Siriman Kanda Touré also laughed. They said, "Manden is now complete." They said they had put their trust in Turama'an. (This is why you sometimes hear a person say that they put their trust in Turama'an instead of Fakoli.[140] The people gave their trust to Turama'an while Fakoli was off visiting his uncle.)

Still standing on the threshold of the council hall, Fakoli said, "Simbon, I do not want a wife from Manden or Negeboriya. Send a message to your uncles in Dò ni Kiri, and ask them to give you your 'nephew wife.'[141] Then give that wife to me. I want to have that woman before we go to the battle at Dakajalan. Then, regardless of what happens, no one will be able to blame my actions in battle on the fact that I have no wife. If I don't have a wife before going into battle, the people will say I fought well because I was trying to

---

138. In the same way that Keleya Konkon could be a classificatory "daughter" of Sumaworo (n. 137), she could also be a classificatory "sister." Indeed, on one path a person can be classified as one's sibling, while on another path the same person can be referred to as one's father, uncle, mother, or aunt. This reflects the polygymous practice of men marrying wives of the same age as their children.

139. The slave would run behind the horse, hanging on to its tail.

140. Turama'an had acquired a leadership position or military command that was formerly held by Fakoli.

141. In Maninka and Bamana society, it is claimed, both jokingly and seriously, that it is the uncle's duty to give his nephew a wife, the so-called "nephew wife." The obligation of this uncle-nephew bond is implied in the Bamana proverb: "When your uncle fails to give you a wife, he is no longer your uncle but your mother's brother."

get myself a wife—that I was afraid of staying a bachelor. So let me have your 'nephew wife' before we leave for the war." Ma'an Sunjata sent a message to his uncle (our ancestor!) in Dò ni Kiri, who sent Ma Sira Condé to Sunjata as his nephew wife. Ma'an Sunjata then gave this wife to Fakoli.

At that time, Fakoli was feeling bitter. Having refused to live in Negeboriya, Manden, and Soso, he'd built his own hamlet and remained there until it was time for the battle at Dakajalan. The people all said, "Eeeh, Fakoli is bitter! He has refused to live with us; he's built his own hamlet." (That hamlet, built in Manden, became Bambugu, and it was there that Sira Condé was brought to Fakoli.)

A VISIT TO KAMANJAN IN SIBI

Dressed in his ritual attire, Sunjata said to Fakoli, "Before she died, my mother asked God to help me earn the support of a Mande elder whose *dalilu* is greater than mine, and I believe I must not go to war without having first accomplished this. Now that you're settled, Fakoli, I ask you—just as I'm asking Turama'an, Kankejan, Tombonon Sitafa Diawara, and all the Simbons—please give me sixty men so I can greet Kamanjan, because I esteem him above all other elders."

Kamanjan was much older than Sunjata; Kamanjan and Sunjata's father, Maghan Konfara, were born at the same time. Kamanjan never committed a shameful deed in his entire life, and anyone who commanded an army would seek his advice. This is why Sunjata said, "Let's go to greet Kamanjan."

With sixty men, Sunjata went to salute Kamanjan at the battle site called Kalassa, near Sibi Mountain, where Kamanjan liked to hold torchlit meetings at night. It was a special honor to be asked by Kamanjan to extinguish the torches at the end of such meetings; only those *kamalenw* he knew to be special in their towns would be allowed to put out the flames.

Sunjata arrived as Kamanjan was having one of his nighttime meetings, and all of the torches were lit. With his hand, Sunjata extinguished them all. Then he used a little thing to reignite them, *kan!* Suddenly everything was illuminated again. The people at the meeting said, "As soon as Sunjata put out the torches, he lit his own torch."

(Sunjata's own light was as powerful as the light from a pressure lamp, and the little town where Sunjata extinguished the torches is called Kalassa, which is near Tabon on the Bamako road. The Konaté live there.)

After relighting the torches, Sunjata saluted Kamanjan and explained the purpose of his visit, saying, "I left here with my mother; now I have returned."

Kamanjan said, "Simbon! Have you come?"

"Yes, I have come."

"Ah, are you the one that Manden will send against Sumaworo?"

"Uhuh. That is why I have come to greet you, father Kamanjan. The last person to be told you're leaving on a trip must be the first person you greet upon your return."

"Sunjata, what *dalilu* did you bring with you? Hm? Sumaworo is a bad one. Haven't you heard people sing his praises? They sing:

> 'Transforms in the air,
> Sumaworo,
> Transforms on the ground,
> Sumaworo.
> Manden pi-pa-pi,
> Whirlwind of Manden,
> Kukuba and Bantamba,
> Nyemi-Nyemi and Kambasiga,
> Sege and Babi'?"

Sunjata said, "Yes, Father Kamanjan, I've heard that."

"Then what kind of *dalilu* did you bring to use against him?"

"Ah, father Kamanjan, that is why I have come to greet you and tell you my thoughts."

"Well, I've become old since we last met here. I can't go to war again, nor can I ask anyone else to do that. All those who attacked Sumaworo have been defeated, and this is Manden's fault; it was Manden that made it possible for Sumaworo to become what he is. It was a mistake for us to give him the four *jamanaw*.[142] Not satisfied with that, he now wants to add Manden to Soso. That is what we must fight to avoid."

Kamanjan and Sunjata were talking beneath the tree that is called *balansan*[143] in Manden, and when Kamanjan said, "Ah!" the *balansan* flipped upside down onto its top branches.

When Sunjata also said, "Ah!" the *balansan* flipped back over onto its roots. (It's true, *binani tinima!*)

Kamanjan said, "Ah!" a second time, and the *balansan* flipped back over onto its top branches.

Before Sunjata could say, "Ah," again, his sister whispered in his ear, "Big brother, this is not what my mother told you to do. Let Kamanjan do this. Our mother prayed that you would be blessed by an elder with *dalilu* stronger than yours. Kamanjan is trying to demonstrate to you how strong his *dalilu* is. If you beat him with your own *dalilu*, he will not give you anything. Let him do this, and he will flip the tree back once he's satisfied. If you add his *dalilu* to what you already have, maybe you will win the war against Sumaworo. You should act like you do not know anything, so Kamanjan will give you his *dalilu*."

---

142. The four main provinces of Soso that commonly appear in praise-lines to Sumaworo (though rarely identified in the same way): Kukuba, Bantamba, Nyemi-Nyemi, and Kambasiga. This comment, which the bard attributes to a contemporary of Sunjata's father, appears to imply a failed policy of appeasement toward Sumaworo.

143. *Acacia albida*; in Mande lore, one of the many trees, including the baobab and the dubalen, that carry strong associations with the spirit world.

A STRATEGIC ALLIANCE: KOLONKAN'S MARRIAGE

The battle that followed Sunjata's meeting with Kamanjan did not go well for Manden, and the town was filled with sorrow. But Kamanjan didn't let Sunjata leave him empty-handed. Kamanjan said, "Simbon, I see that your sister has matured since we last met. Yes, she has matured, and you should give her to me so I can marry her. Though your sister spent twenty-seven years at Nema, your mother—who was of the best stock—said she would never be given to a man there. You yourself agreed that your sister would only be married here in Manden. So give her to me."

Ma'an Sunjata said, "Eh! Father Kamanjan, that won't be possible. If I give you my younger sister, I would be embarrassed to discuss certain subjects with you. There are things I could discuss with you so long as there's no marriage between us. Now that my mother and father are both dead, I'm depending on your counsel on such matters. But a marriage between us would make it embarrassing for me to do so.[144] Besides that, you are a battle commander. If we do something to displease you, if you become offended, we might quarrel."

Kamanjan said, "Ah, give her to me."

"Well, I'll give her to you if you will command the Kamara people to show respect for the Mansaré people. Tell the Kamara people to show respect for my people and for me. The Kamara should respect us, *Kamaralu yé dan a na.*" (The Dannalu, who take their name from that saying, live between Balia and Wulada. Now, because of Ma Kolonkan's marriage to Kamanjan, the Dannalu must be mentioned whenever the

---

144. In this case of *buranya* ("having an older in-law"), Sunjata would have to practice great restraint and lack of familiarity toward his sister's husband, and would no longer be able to appeal to him for help or advice.

Kamara are discussed.) Ma Kolonkan was given to Kamanjan Kamara as soon as he made this promise to Sunjata. Kamanjan entered her, and she eventually gave birth to his son Fadibali.

THE BATTLE OF NEGEBORIYA

Kamanjan said, "Simbon, I respect you, and believe you'll be successful in the war against Sumaworo. But listen: don't go to Dakajalan yet. Go to Negeboriya first and pay your respects to Fakoli's relatives. Though Fakoli is from Negeboriya, not Manden, he has done much for us. Besides, haven't you ever heard the saying, 'Negeboriya Maghan, Kayafaya Maghan'?[145] The Negeboriyans are our in-laws.

"Fakoli has said, 'The Mande people are wrong if they think I am helping them only because I want to win the *mansaya* for myself,' and we believe him. After all, none of the Koroma living in our Mansaré towns have ever tried to take the *mansaya* for themselves.

"Fakoli has also said, 'I am only helping Manden because of Ma Tenenba Condé; it was she who raised and blessed me. Tenenba Condé's sister is So'olon Wulen Condé, and So'olon Wulen Condé's son is Ma'an Sunjata. So I am not helping you because of personal ambition. If you listen to the Mande people's gossip about me now, you'll be ashamed to face me later.'

"Turama'an and Kankejan have said the same sorts of things. So go and pay your respects to the people of Negeboriya."

Taking their leave from Tabon, Ma'an Sunjata and his companions mounted their horses and rode straight to

---

145. Kayafaya is said to have been a *jamana*, or province attached to Negeboriya under the Koroma ruling lineage.

Negeboriya. But Sumaworo had built a wall around that town by the time they arrived. In fact, Sumaworo had built walls around many towns of Manden and was occupying them with his troops.

When Sumaworo's men heard that So'olon Ma'an and his troops were coming to pay their respects to the people of Negeboriya, they lined their musket barrels along the top of the wall and waited. When Sunjata and his men arrived, the muskets fired and fired and fired at them!

Forced to retreat, Sunjata returned to find Manden in mourning over his defeat at the Battle of Negeboriya. But Sunjata's powerful army was not destroyed, and Sumaworo had lost his sacred drum Dunun Mutukuru during the battle. (That drum, the Dunun Mutukuru, was never found; only the *bala* was saved.)

[In omitted passages, back in Manden two rams that are named for Sunjata and Sumaworo, respectively, fight one another in a symbolic preview of the battle to come. Preparing for the Battle of Dakajalan, Sunjata calls for volunteers. The army of Manden is divided into companies of men who possess occult powers, companies of those who have no magic, and one unit made up of famous ancestral figures with the power to become invisible. In a secret meeting with Manjan Bereté, Sunjata learns the elaborate strategy he must adopt to defeat Sumaworo. He exchanges his sorcery horse for the sorcery mare of the jelimuso *Tunku Manyan Diawara. He also sends a messenger to his sister, Nana Triban, who is in Soso, to retrieve from her the* dibilan *medicine that she steals from the tail of Sumaworo's horse.]*

TRADING INSULTS AND
SWEARING OATHS

Manden mourned after each of their battles against
Sumaworo. He made many women widows. He made shirts
and pants from the skins of Mande and Soso people. He
sewed a hat of human skin. He even made shoes of human
skin and then ordered the surviving Mande people to come
and name them. If one of the people tried to name the
shoes "Finfirinya Shoes," Sumaworo would say, "That is not
the name." If someone tried "Dulubiri shoes," he would say,
"That is not the name." Finally, the people asked him, "All
right, Sumaworo, what are your shoes called?" He said, "My
human-skin shoes are called 'Take the Air, take the Ground
from the Chief.' I wear your skins because the Mande people
will always be around me, Sumaworo. You will always be in
my power."

After both sides had made their preparations, the war
began. Briefly, here's what happened:

The three Mande divisions—including those men who
could become invisible in the daytime and the five *mori* diviners—arrived at the first battle. Simbon was placed in the middle of his men, with Manjan Bereté directly in front of him.
The men were packed so tightly that the head of one man's
horse touched the tail of the horse in front of him. Sanbari
Mara Cissé and Siriman Kanda Touré were there, as were Kòn
Mara and Djané, Manden Bori, Tombonon Sitafa Diawara,
Turama'an, Kankejan, and Fakoli. Sunjata ordered them to
maintain their positions on the battlefield, so they marched
back and forth in a line, like an army of ants. Simbon was in
the middle!

When they arrived at the battlefield, Ma'an Sunjata said,
"Men of Manden, wait here," and crossed the field with
his masked flag bearers, headed for Sumaworo's camp.
Sumaworo's troops were also there, waiting in position.

Sumaworo sat astride his horse, surrounded by his corps of personal guards.

As he approached Sumaworo, Sunjata said, "Father Sumaworo, good morning." (True bravery is revealed by the mouth!)

Sumaworo said, "Marahaba, good morning. Where are the Mande troops?"

"Ah, Father Sumaworo, they are over on the Mande side."

"Ah, is that how you usually arrange your troops?"

Sunjata said, "Well, I am new at this. This is our first encounter in battle. If I brought my men over here, they'd mingle with your troops, and we'd be unable to tell whose men are whose.[146] You can see them standing over there on the Mande side."

"Ah, So'olon Ma'an, this is not the usual procedure."

Feeling bold, Sunjata said, "Well, you killed all of the other leaders; there was nobody left to lead the Mande troops."

Sumaworo said, "I say to you, Bala Fasali, tell Simbon that I am doing him a favor by inviting him to meet here on the battlefield. I understand that the Mande people sent for Sunjata so he could be their commander in battle. But apparently they did not tell him about anything that happened while he was away.

"This is why I have invited him to come and meet in the field: so that I can tell him what I have to say, and he can tell me what is on his mind. Then I will do to him what I planned to do—or he can try to do to me what he wants to."

Simbon said, "I appreciate the invitation. Ah! You are my respected elder. The person who has helped one's father is also one's father. But let me tell you something, father Sumaworo: people may refuse peanuts, but not the ones that have been placed right in front of them."

---

146. The problem of distinguishing between ally and enemy in the heat of battle was a serious concern. In an episode not included in this book, the narrator describes how Kamanjan Kamara introduced facial scarification for that purpose.

Sumaworo said, "M'ba, give me some snuff from Manden."[147]

"Ah! Father Sumaworo, it is more appropriate for the master to give snuff to his apprentice, rather than for the apprentice to give snuff to his master. Give me some snuff from Soso, so that I will know I have met my master."

Sumaworo took out his snuffbox and handed it to Sunjata. Simbon put some snuff in his palm, took a pinch and snorted it, took another pinch and snorted it, and put some in his mouth. He closed the snuffbox and gave it back to Sumaworo. The snuff did not even make Sunjata's tongue quiver.

Sumaworo was surprised. Anybody who took that snuff would immediately fall over. It was poison! But So'olon Ma'an sucked on the snuff and didn't even cough. He spit the snuff on the ground.

Then Sumaworo said, "Give me some Mande snuff." Simbon reached in his pocket, took out his snuffbox, and handed it to Sumaworo, who put some in his palm. He took a pinch of snuff and snorted it, took some more and snorted it, and put the rest in his mouth. That was specially prepared snuff, too, but it did not do anything to him.

Sumaworo said to him, "I asked you to meet with me because the Mande people seem to think you are their *mansa*, and it's true that you would not be here if you didn't have some *dalilu*. But your *dalilu* will do no good against me. I told you before, when you passed through Soso, that if the Mande people tried to send you to fight me, you should refuse. As you now know, I have become hot ashes surrounding Manden and Soso; any toddler who tries to cross me will be burned up to his thighs. And yet here you are."

"Ah, father Sumaworo, as I told you, this is my father's home, not yours. You are not from here: your grandfather came from Folonengbe; your father was a latecomer to Manden. You are only the second generation of your people

_____

147. This request commences a standard ritual called *sigifili*, conducted between opposing commanders before a battle; it involved boasting about one's powers and swearing oaths while taking a poisonous snuff that would kill a liar.

in Manden. But we have been here for eight generations: our ancestor Mamadi Kani first came here from Hejaji.[148] After him came Mamadi Kani's son, Kani Simbon, Kani Nyogo Simbon, Kabala Simbon, Big Simbon Mamadi Tanyagati, Balinene, Bele, and Belebakòn, and Farako Manko Farakonken. Now I am Farako Manko Farakonken's son, the eighth generation. My people have been here all along; you only arrived yesterday, your dawn is just breaking today.

"Huh!" continued Sunjata. "And you say that I have just arrived? M'ba, huh! You are my respected elder, so I will not be the first to make a move. You invited me here to tell me that I'm a disrespectful child? You just go ahead and show what you've got."

Sumaworo said, "Bisimillahi."

THE BATTLE OF DAKAJALAN AND FAKOLI'S REVENGE

When something is filled to the brim, it will overflow.

When Sumaworo took his sword and struck at Sunjata, his blade flexed like a whip. Sunjata also struck with his sword; the blade of his sword also bent. Sumaworo raised his musket and fired, but nothing touched So'olon Ma'an. So'olon Ma'an then fired his musket at Sumaworo but failed to wound him.

With that, the *dalilu* was finished, and the two men just stood there. Sumaworo reached into his saddlebag and took his whip. As he raised his hand like this, So'olon Ma'an seized his reins like this—*Clap!*—and dashed away.

---

148. Hejaji: see n. 31; Mamadi Kani: see n. 120.

The two armies were waiting, Soso on one side, Manden on the other. Everybody was watching the commanders on the battlefield. Fakoli stood off to one side of Sunjata; Turama'an was on his other side. Sumaworo was also flanked by his men.

Blu, blu! Sunjata, Sumaworo, and their men dashed across the field and up the hill. Near the top of the hill, they faded from sight; even their dust disappeared. Soon they reached the edge of a very deep ravine. Gathering all her strength, Sunjata's sorcery mare (Tunku Manyan Diawara's horse) jumped the ravine and landed on the other side. When Sumaworo's horse tried to jump the ravine, it tumbled to the bottom.[149] Fakoli and Turama'an—whose horses safely jumped the ravine—turned and, with Sunjata, went to look down at Sumaworo who was trapped at the bottom of the ravine.

Sunjata called down, "Sumaworo, what is the matter?"

"So'olon Ma'an, kill me here; do not carry me to the town. Do not bring such shame to me. God controls all time. Please do not take me back."

Sumaworo removed his *dalilu* and dropped his horse-whip. He stripped completely, taking off his human-skin shirt and trousers.

Sunjata said, "I am not going to finish you off. No one can climb out of that ravine; you're stuck. I do not want your shirt of human skin, because it is the skin of my father's relatives. I will not take it." Turning to his companions he said, "Come, let's go home."

They had gone some distance when Fakoli made a decision, turned, and went back to the ravine. When he arrived there, he said to Sumaworo, "What did I tell you? When you took back your sister,[150] what did I say?" Taking his axe from his shoulder, Fakoli struck Sumaworo on the head, *poh!* He said, "This will be mentioned in Ma'an Sunjata's praise song."

---

149. Though not usually seen in versions of the Sunjata epic, the incident of the horse tumbling into a ravine is a popular motif in *jeli* storytelling, a favorite way of disposing of the hero's enemy.

150. Fakoli's wife, Keleya Konkon (see pp. xxi and 108–9).

(And he was right! Though we sing, "Head-breaking Mari Jata," it was Fakoli who broke Sumaworo's head.)[151]

Fakoli started to leave. But he was still angry, so he went back to the ravine again and struck Sumaworo on the leg, *gbao!* Fakoli broke Sumaworo's leg, saying, "This will also be mentioned in Ma'an Sunjata's praise song." (That is why we sing, "Leg-Breaking Mari Jata.")

With his axe, Fakoli returned to the ravine a third time and broke Sumaworo's arm, saying, "This, too, will be mentioned in Ma'an Sunjata's praise song." (And so we sing, "Arm-Breaking Mari Jata." Aheh! It was not Jata who broke it! It was Fakoli who broke it.)

Finally Sunjata and his men went home. Laughter returned to Manden, and eventually Soso joined in.

[In omitted passages, the narrator describes how, following the defeat of Sumaworo, the people of Soso dispersed and eventually settled in various communities along the Atlantic coast. Meanwhile, Sunjata begins to initiate reforms and organize the newly unified Mali Empire.]

---

151. It is unusual for a *jeli* to describe the death of Sumaworo, as Tassey Condé does here. In many versions, Sumaworo flees to the mountain at Koulikoro where he disappears. The Kouyaté and Diabaté *jeliw*, among others, are usually careful not to say that Sumaworo was slain by Sunjata, Fakoli, or anybody else. Such things are taken seriously in modern times, because Maninka and Bamana identify with the ancestors whose names they carry. The version translated here was recorded in a private performance in the narrator's own house, but in a public performance, giving details of a humiliating defeat (even one alleged to have occurred more than seven centuries ago) risks embarrassing any people in the audience who regard themselves as descendants of the defeated ancestor.

THE CAMPAIGN AGAINST JOLOFIN MANSA

After the war was over, Ma'an Sunjata said, "My fathers and my brothers: now that the war has ended and the *mansaya* has come to us, the Mansaré, let's send our horse-buyers to Senu to replace the many Mande horses killed by Sumaworo. We should buy enough horses for each of our elders and warriors to have one."

So the horse-buyers went to Senu and bought hundreds of horses. On the way back to Manden, the horse-buyers stopped at the *jamana* of Jolofin Mansa, and there Jolofin Mansa robbed the buyers of their horses; he then took the horse-buyers captive and beheaded all but two. Jolofin Mansa sent the two survivors to tell Ma'an Sunjata that even though Ma'an Sunjata had taken over the power—that Sunjata had recently received the Mande *mansaya*—he knew the Mande walked on all fours like dogs, and that they should leave horse-riding to others.

The two horse-buyers arrived in Manden and gave the message to Ma'an Sunjata, who said, "Jolofin Mansa has extended an invitation to me. I myself will lead the campaign against Jolofin Mansa."

His younger brother Manden Bori said, "Elder brother, are you going to lead us in that campaign? Give me the command, and I will do the fighting."

"I am not giving you command of the army."

Fakoli said, "Simbon, give me the army! We will not stay here while you lead the army. Give the army to me, Fakoli, so I can go after Jolofin Mansa."

Simbon said, "I will not give you the army. I will go myself."

Meanwhile, Turama'an was digging his own grave. He cut some *tòrò* branches, laid them on his grave, and had his shroud sewn. Then he said to Ma'an Sunjata, "Simbon, I'll kill myself if you do not give me the army. Would you really leave us behind while you lead the army to go after Jolofin Mansa? Give me the army. If you don't, if you go after Jolofin Mansa yourself, you will lose me, for I'll kill myself."

"Ah," said Simbon. "I did not know you felt so strongly, Turama'an. Your *dalilu* and my *dalilu* are tied together: my mother was given to your fathers, who killed the buffalo of Dò ni Kiri. If your father and my mother had gotten along, my mother would have stayed with your father. Because my mother did not get along with your fathers, your fathers brought my mother to my father, and I was born out of that marriage, as were my younger brothers Manden Bori and So'olon Jamori.

"My father took my younger siblings Nana Triban and Tenenbajan, and gave them to Danmansa Wulanni and Danmansa Wulanba, your fathers. You, Turama'an, are the son of Danmansa Wulanni. Considering what you have said, you and I are equal in this war, and I will let you take the army."

So Sunjata gave Turama'an command of the army, and Turama'an prepared the army for war. With the campaign underway, they marched to Jolofin Mansa's land.

(You know Jolofin Mansa, he was one of the Mansaré. The son of Latali Kalabi, the Mansaré ancestor, was Danmatali Kalabi; Danmatali Kalabi then also named his son Latali Kalabi. This second Latali sired Kalabi Doman and Kalabi Bomba, and Kalabi Doman sired Mamadi Kani. Mamadi Kani sired Kani Simbon, Kani Nyogo Simbon, Kabala Simbon, Big Simbon Madi Tanyagati, and M'balinene; M'balinene sired Bele, Bele sired Belebakon, Belebakon sired Maghan Konfara, and this Farako Manko Farakonken was Ma'an Sunjata's father.

So Jolofin *Mansa* and Ma'an Sunjata both descended from the same person. And Jolofin's people—the *Jolofin na mò'òlu*—became known as the Wolofo.[152] Have you heard people

---

152. Maninka pronunciation attaches an extra vowel. The Wolof, who call their country Jolof (see previous sentence), are mainly in Senegal (the narrator's "Senu"), and they speak a language that is not interintelligible with Manding languages.

calling the Wolofo "little Mande people"? That's because they all came from Manden.)

Turama'an marched the army of Manden to Jolofin Mansa's land and there destroyed Jolofin Mansa's place like it was an old clay pot; Turama'an broke it like an old calabash. He also captured those who were supposed to be captured, killed those who were supposed to be killed.

Though his soldiers had been defeated, Jolofin Mansa had not been captured, so he fled with Turama'an in pursuit. Jolofin Mansa headed for the big river.[153]

At that time, no one knew that Jolofin Mansa could transform himself into a crocodile, living on land or under water. When he came to the big river, Jolofin Mansa plunged in and swam into a cave; there he transformed himself into a crocodile and lay down to wait.

Standing above the cave, Turama'an and his men said, "Jolofin Mansa went in here." The Mande men were good warriors, but they were not used to water fighting. All of the battle commanders standing there were dressed for fighting on land; they were all wearing hunting clothes and carried quivers and bows. Until they stood at the entrance to that cave, the Mande people did not know that they had a warrior who could fight under water.

Turama'an said, "Jolofin Mansa has changed himself into a crocodile and gone into that cave. We can't leave him there, for if we destroy the war *mansa's* home without killing the war *mansa* himself, we have not won the battle. But who will go after him?"

Everybody kept quiet, *lele*!

Again Turama'an asked, "Who will go after him?" Nobody spoke up, so Turama'an asked a third time, "Who will follow this man?"

The Diawara chief, whose name was Tombonon Sitafa Diawara, stepped out from among the soldiers. He said, "Turama'an, tell the Mande people that if they agree, I, Sitafa Diawara, will go after Jolofin Mansa. But also tell them that I

---

153. The Senegal River.

am not doing this to prove my manhood. I'm doing it because we can"t return home to Simbon having only destroyed Jolofin Mansa's home. If we return home without also having killed Jolofin Mansa himself, Simbon will wonder why we told him to stay home."

(That is why, if you are a real man, you should stay low to the ground when you are among the *kamalenw*. You should only reveal the kind of man you are when somebody challenges your group.)

Meanwhile, Jolofin Mansa's crocodile wraith was lying in the cave, its mouth open wide. The upper jaw reached to the top of the entrance, the lower jaw reached to the bottom. Anybody who went after the crocodile would end up in its stomach, and the crocodle would just close his mouth. Eh! There would be no need to chew.

Sitafa Diawara said, "I'll give you two signs when I get down to where the crocodile is. If, while the water is bubbling and churning and turning the color of blood, you see a pelican flying from where the sun sets to where it rises, Manden should weep, for you'll know that Jolofin Mansa has defeated me. But if, while the water is bubbling and churning and turning the color of blood, the pelican flies from where the sun rises to where it sets, you Mande people should be happy, for it will mean I have honored you and God. Those are the signs I've given you."

Diawara put on his medicine clothes and gathered all his *dalilu.* He had a small knife fastened to his chest, and a short Bozo[154] fish-spear hung from his waist.

To the other warriors Diawara said, "Excuse me. We may meet in this world or we may meet in God's kingdom. If I'm successful, we'll meet in this world; I'll come back and find you here. But if I'm overcome by the crocodile, we'll meet in God's kingdom." Then he dove into the water and swam into the cave, unaware that he was actually swimming straight

---

154. An ethnic group of the Middle Niger, specializing in fishing and boating occupations, mainly located between Sansanding and Lake Debo in Mali.

into the crocodile's stomach. The crocodile closed its mouth on him.

As the crocodile closed its mouth on him, Diawara the hunter demonstrated his *dalilu*. Though he was trapped inside the crocodile, he was still alive, as comfortable as if he were in his own house. Taking his spear from his side, he stabbed the crocodile here, *pu!*; he stabbed it there, *pu!* The crocodile went *kututu*. Diawara speared the crocodile over and over again.

The water bubbled, and blood came to the surface. As the water around him turned bloody, Diawara reached for the knife on his chest. He sliced a hole in the crocodile's belly and swam out of it. Then, still under the water, he twisted the crocodile's front legs and tied them together.

As Diawara swam to the surface with the crocodile, a pelican flew by, squawking, from east to west. Manden laughed. As they hauled the crocodile wraith up onto the riverbank, Jolofin Mansa himself appeared. He was captured, tied up, and taken to Sunjata, the *mansa*.

Turama'an, who was the commander at that battle, brought Jolofin Mansa's treasure to Ma'an Sunjata. Manden was at last free, and the war was over.

EPILOGUE

After describing the defeat of Sumaworo and the successful campaign against Jolofin Mansa, some of the most knowledgeable *jeliw* include descriptions of a great assembly held at a large open space called Kurukanfuwa. They generally claim it was there that Sunjata laid the groundwork for administering the newly established Mali Empire, including the assignment of provincial governorships to his leading generals. Among those who mention the assembly at Kurukanfuwa is our narrator Tassey Condé, who presents it as the occasion for efforts to shape the social framework of Manding peoples. He claims that quarrels over who had rights to the services of *jeliw*, blacksmiths, leatherworkers, potters, and other occupational specialists were settled at Kurukanfuwa. In this bard's view, the solution was to assign a special social classification to the artists and craftsmen, who became collectively known as *nyamakalaw*, and to award their services to the most worthy and successful families of Manden.

Aside from the fact that Tassey Condé's basic narrative required six days to complete (more was added in subsequent interviews), it is unusual because it continues for several thousand lines after the fall of Sumaworo and Jolofin Mansa. Tassey revisits subjects mentioned earlier in the narrative and provides a wealth of additional details and explanations about them. A few such details appear in the "Introduction" and explanatory notes, such as the origins and occupation of Sumaworo's ancestors in the place called Folonengbe, and remarks about the absence of guns in the time of Sunjata. Subjects that did not find a place in the present book include details about the "original" five Islamic lineages of Manden and the towns where they settled, the iron-working communities of Negeboriya, Fakoli's genealogy and descendants, the Koroma lineage's dispersal and towns they founded, Manden's first pilgrims to Mecca, Manden Bori's descendants and where they settled, history of Sankaran, five branches of the Kulubali of Segu, leading families of Kouroussa and the Hamana region, Dò ni Kiri's war with Sawuru, early settlers in various regions to the south of Manden, Baté and Kankan history with the Nabé and Kaba as latecomers from Diafunu, the four *jamanaw* of Soso, the Soso people's diaspora, ancestry of the Magasouba of Siguiri and their *dalilu*, more on the history of the Kaba of Kankan, background on the Konaté of the *jamana* of Toron, and Kamanjan's famous meeting at Kalassa.

Follow-up interviews with Tassey Condé and the elders of Fadama elicited more discourse, revealing additional detailed information on a variety of subjects. The entire corpus of discourse on the Condé perception of the Manding peoples' history will be included in the complete, exhaustively annotated scholarly edition being prepared for publication under the title *Great Sogolon's House.*

GLOSSARY OF FREQUENTLY USED MANINKA TERMS

Note: The suffixes "w" and "lu" are alternatively used to signify the plural—e.g., jeliw *or* jelilu.

bala   Also known as *balafon*, the indigenous xylophone. Constructed of hardwood slats tied to a bamboo frame with small gourds attached below each slat for resonance. Played with wooden mallets, the heads of which are covered with liquid latex tapped from wild rubber trees.

balansan   In Manding lore, one of the trees that carries strong associations with genies and the spirit world.

dabali   A scheme or a plan. As a verb, to make something happen in a positive way—e.g., to repair; also, secret power sometimes used in negative ways—e.g., "the sorcerer will *dabali* him so he will not be able to walk."

dado   Dried hibiscus blossoms and/or leaves, used as a condiment in sauces.

dalilu   According to the context usually seen in oral tradition, magic, or occult power; more generally, any means used to achieve a goal, referring to secret power, whether supernatural or not. Someone might have the *dalilu* to bring rain, but also used in casual daily usage—e.g., "he has the *dalilu* to repair a car," or "I have no *dalilu* to interfere in that quarrel."

gbensen   An old unit of trade currency made of thick strands of iron wire bent into the shape of a cross.

jamana   Land, territory, province; in Maninka oral tradition: chiefdom, kingdom; Bamana syn. *kafu.*

jamu   Family name, patronymic, identity.

jeli (pl. jeliw/jelilu)   Occupationally defined bard (popularly and more broadly known as "griot"), born into the profession, specializing in speech including genealogies, proverbs, and extended oral narrative, also vocal and instrumental music.

jelimuso   Female bard (*muso* = "woman," "wife," "female"), specializing in praise-singing and vocalization of songs from the vast Mande repertoire.

jeliya   Condition of being a *jeli* or *jelimuso.*

kamalen   Male youth distinguished by two categories: *kamalennin* = adolescent; circumcised youth; vigorous young males 15–25 years of age; *kamalenkoro* = a mature male at the height of his power and ability, 25–40 years of age. The most physically capable social ranks, from which came the hunters, warriors, champion farmers, and long-distance traders.

karamogo   Teacher, scholar, wise man; as a proper noun, Karamogo is both a given name and an honorific for learned men, usually Muslim clerics.

kora   Largest of the calabash harps, with twenty-one strings.

kòwòro   A musical instrument also known as *dan* or *ndan*, consisting of an inverted open calabash with a neck for each of its six strings; technically known as a pentatonic pluriac.

maghan   See *mansa.*

mansa   Ruler, king, chief, lord, emperor (syn. *magha* or *maghan*).

mansaya   Kingship, royalty, the condition of being a ruler.

marahaba   Response to a greeting that honors people by saluting their ancestors with the family name or *jamu* (patronymic, identity). From Ar. *mrehba* ("welcome").

m'ba   Contraction of *marahaba*, but used as a figure of speech (like "well" or "okay") or a standard response to virtually any remark.

mori   In general, a Muslim cleric (Fr. *marabout*), but in oral tradition often referring to a seer or diviner who draws on spiritual connections with both the indigenous system of belief and Islam.

naamu From the Arabic *na'am*. Most often used as a reply or comment by the *naamu*-sayer (*naamu namina*, or *naamutigiw* = *naamu* "owner"), who encourages the principal performer. There is no very accurate translation, though it is what people also say when they hear their name called, and it can be rendered as "yes," or "I hear you."

nege "Iron"—syn. *nkarinyan*: a rhythm instrument consisting of a notched iron tube 7–8 inches long, held in one hand and scraped with a thin metal rod. It is often played to accompany the hunters' or youth harps.

nkoni A type of traditional lute consisting of four to five strings attached to a single neck on a wooden, trough-shaped body covered with animal skin.

sunsun An extremely hard wood called "false ebony" or "West African ebony."

MAJOR CHARACTERS

Abdu Karimi   Son of Abdu Serifu, the king of Morocco. Younger of the two brothers who hunted the Buffalo of Dò ni Kiri, and the one who actually killed it. Subsequently known by the praise name Danmansa Wulanni.

Abdu Kassimu   Son of Abdu Serifu, the king of Morocco. Elder of the two brothers who hunted the Buffalo of Dò ni Kiri. Subsequently known by the praise name Danmansa Wulanba.

Bala Fasali   Also known as Bala Fasaké, Fasséké, or other variants of that name. Son of Nyankuman Duga who is variously identified as the *jeli* of Sunjata's father, or of Sumaworo. Destined to be the principal *jeli* of Sunjata, Bala was sent to Soso and acquired the traditional xylophone, or *bala*, from Sumaworo. With his father, he is recognized as an ancestor of the great bardic lineage known as Kouyaté.

Dankaran Tuman   Sunjata's rival stepbrother, son of Sansun Bereté and Maghan Konaté of Konfara. He inherited the power from their father, plotted to kill Sunjata, and, as ruler of Manden while Sunjata was in exile, failed to protect his country from Soso invasion and occupation.

Danmansa Wulanba   Formerly known as Abdu Kassimu, elder of the two brothers from Morocco. After his younger brother killed the buffalo of Dò ni Kiri, he sang his praises and consequently became the legendary ancestor of the bardic lineage called Diabaté.

Danmansa Wulanni   Formerly known as Abdu Karimi, younger of the two brothers from Morocco. He killed the buffalo of Dò ni Kiri and became the legendary ancestor of the Tarawèlè (Traoré) lineage.

Dò Kamissa the Buffalo Woman   Stepsister of Donsamogo Diarra, the *mansa* of Dò ni Kiri. She was the elder sister of both Sunjata's mother, Sogolon Wulen Condé, and Fakoli's foster-mother, Tenenba Condé. One of the greatest sorceresses in Manding epic tradition, Kamissa is especially remembered for her ability to transform herself into a buffalo.

Donsamogo Diarra   Full name: Donsamò'ò Nyèmò'ò Diarra, mansa of Dò ni Kiri. He was the son of Ma'an Solonkan and the elder brother of Sekou, Mafadu, and Kiri Diarra, and the three sisters Dò Kamissa, Sogolon, and Tenenba Condé. Upon inheriting the power at Dò ni Kiri, he refused to share the father's legacy with Dò Kamissa.

Fakoli Koroma   Son of Yerelenko Koroma, *mansa* of Negeboriya, and his second wife Kosiya Kanté, who was the sister of Sumaworo of Soso. As a distinguished son of both Soso and Negeboriya, Fakoli was the single most important military ally of Sunjata. He is also recalled as the greatest sorcerer of the male Manding ancestors, and as patriarch of many of the principal blacksmith lineages.

Faran Tunkara   *Mansa* of Nema/Mema, who ruled from his capital of Kuntunya and hosted Sogolon Wulen Condé, her son Sunjata, and his siblings during their years of exile.

Jelimusoni Tunku Manyan Diawara   One of nine *jelimusow* (female bards) married by Maghan Konfara, in his quest to find the mother of Sunjata, and the only one of that group said to have borne a child. She was among the four messengers who traveled to Nema/Mema in search of Sunjata. She was also one of the nine sorceresses bribed by Dankaran Tuman to assassinate Sunjata, and the one who warned him of the plot. She later provided the sorcery mare that Sunjata rode at the Battle of Dakajalan.

Jinna Maghan   Lit. "Genie King," a ubiquitous supernatural being who can appear wherever important events occur involving genies.

Jolofin Mansa   *Mansa* of the Jolof Kingdom of Senegal, who confiscated Sunjata's herd of horses and sent him an insulting message, and was later defeated by an army led by Turama'an Traoré.

Jonmusoni Manyan   One of nine slave girls married by Maghan Konfara in his quest to find the mother of Sunjata, and the only one of that group who is said to have borne a child. She was among the four messengers who traveled to Nema/Mema in search of Sunjata.

Kamanjan Kamara   Full name and title: Tabon Wana Faran Kamara (or Sibi Wana Faran Kamara). The most distinguished ancestor of the Kamara (also Camara) lineage, he was *mansa* of Sibi and Tabon, and a contemporary of Sunjata's father Maghan Konfara. He became an elderly brother-in-law to Sunjata when he married Kolonkan after she and her siblings returned from exile.

Kankejan   Son of Danmansa Wulanba and Tenenbajan, who was a daughter of Maghan Konfara's younger brother. An ancestor of the Diabaté *jeliw*, he was one of Sunjata's important generals and fought at the Battle of Dakajalan.

Keleya Konkon   The wife of Fakoli, who had been given to him by his uncle Sumaworo of Soso. When Sumaworo became aware of Keleya's great power as a sorceress, and after he quarreled with Fakoli, he reclaimed her from his nephew.

Kolonkan   Daughter of Maghan Konfara and Sogolon Wulen Condé, and sister of Sunjata. After she returned from exile with Sunjata, she was married to Kamanjan Kamara of Sibi and gave birth to a son, Fadibali.

Kosiya Kanté   Sister of Sumaworo Kanté, second wife of Mansa Yerelenko of Negeboriya, and mother of Fakoli. She sacrificed herself to Jinna Maghan the genie chief, so her brother could acquire the Soso *bala*.

Maghan Konfara   Husband of Sogolon Wulen Condé, father of Sunjata, generally identified as an ancestor of the Konaté. Full name in this text: Farako Manko Farakonken; identified elsewhere as Naré Maghan Konaté and Naré Famagan, among other variants. He was *mansa* of Konfara, descendant of Latili Kalabi, Mamadi Kani, Kani Simbon, Kaninyo'o Simbon, Kabala Simbon, Big Simbon Madi Tanyagati, M'bali Nèènè, Bèlè, and son of Bèlèbakòn.

Manden Bori   Youngest son of Maghan Konfara and Sogolon Wulen Condé, brother of Sunjata, Kolonkan, and Jamori. He is the ancestor of the chiefly Keita families of the Hamana region of Guinea.

Manjan Bereté   Identified by a place name as Tombonon Manjan Bereté (cf. Sitafa Diawara). Brother of Sansun Tuman Bereté. One of Maghan Konfara's chief advisers, he is recalled as being the leading Muslim of his day. He was one of the four messengers who traveled to Nema/Mema to bring Sunjata back from exile.

Nana Triban   Daughter of Maghan Konfara and Sansun Tuman Bereté, half-sister of Sunjata. She was the wife of Danmansa Wulanni and mother of Turama'an Traoré.

Sansamba Sagado   Chief of the Somono boatmen. He ferried Sogolon and her children across the Niger River when they left Manden to go into exile.

Sansun Bereté   Full name: Sansun Tuman (Sansuma) Bereté. Sister of Tombonon Manjan Bereté, wife of Maghan Konfara, co-wife of Sogolon Wulen Condé, mother of Dankaran Tuman and Nana Triban.

Siriman Kanda Touré   One of Sunjata's important generals. He was one of the four messengers who journeyed to Nema/Mema in search of Sunjata, and he later fought at the Battle of Dakajalan.

Sitafa Diawara   Identified as Tombonon Sitafa Diawara. He was one of Sunjata's important generals and fought at the Battle of Dakajalan. Later, on the campaign against Jolofin Mansa, he was the hero who followed Jolofin Mansa's crocodile wraith into the underwater cave and emerged triumphant.

Sogolon Wulen Condé   Daughter of Ma'an Solonkan, *mansa* of Dò ni Kiri. She was a sister of both Dò Kamissa the Buffalo Woman and Tenenba Condé. A formidable sorceress, she became the wife of Maghan Konfara and gave birth to Sunjata, Kolonkan, Jamori, and Manden Bori.

So'olon Jamori   Second son of Maghan Konfara and Sogolon Wulen Condé. As the middle brother (some say he was a half-brother), he was younger than Sunjata and older than Manden Bori. He was killed in an ambush when he and his siblings were leaving Nema/Mema on their return journey from exile.

So'olon Kolonkan   See *Kolonkan.*

Sumaworo Kanté   Son of Bali Kanté, he was the *mansa* of Soso. He is associated with the origin of Manding stringed instruments, as well as the Soso *bala*, which he is said to have acquired from the genies. Taking advantage of the weakness of Dankaran Tuman, he conquered the formerly autonomous Mande chiefdoms and occupied them while Sunjata was in exile.

Sunjata Keita   Also known as So'olon Jara (Sogolon's Lion), So'olon Ma'an, Ma'an Sunjata, Mari Jata, Danama Yirindi, Simbon, and other praise names. Son of Maghan Konfara and Sogolon Wulen Condé. He was leader of the army of Manden when it defeated Sumaworo and the army of Soso, and is generally credited as "founder" of the Mali Empire.

Tenenba Condé   Also known as Soma Tenenba or Ma Tenenba. Daughter of Ma'an Solonkan, the *mansa* of Dò ni Kiri; sister of Dò Kamissa and Sogolon Wulen Condé. She was the first wife of Yerelenko, *mansa* of Negeboriya, co-wife of Kosiya Kanté, and foster mother of Fakoli.

Tenenbajan Konaté   Daughter of a younger brother of Maghan Konfara. She was the wife of Danmansa Wulanba and the mother of Kankejan, who was an ancestor of the Diabaté *jeliw.*

Turama'an Traoré (Tarawele)   Also Turamaghan, Tirmakan, and so on. Son of Danmansa Wulanni and Nana Triban. As one of Sunjata's most important generals, he fought at the Battle of Dakajalan, and after the defeat of Soso he commanded the campaign against Jolofin Mansa.

Yerelenko Koroma   *Mansa* of Negeboriya, which was probably the most important iron-producing region of Manden. His senior wife was Tenenba Condé of Dò ni Kiri. He became the brother-in-law of Sumaworo when he married Kosiya Kanté of Soso, who was the mother of his son Fakoli.

SUGGESTIONS FOR FURTHER READING

Austen, Ralph A., ed. *In Search of Sunjata: The Mande Epic as History, Literature, and Performance.* Bloomington and Indianapolis: Indiana University Press, 1999.

Barber, Karin, and P. F. de Moraes Farias, eds. *Discourse and Its Disguises: The Interpretation of African Oral Texts.* Birmingham, UK: Centre of West African Studies, University of Birmingham, 1989.

Belcher, Stephen. *Epic Traditions of Africa.* Bloomington and Indianapolis: Indiana University Press, 1999.

Brett-Smith, Sarah C. *The Making of Bamana Sculpture: Creativity and Gender.* Cambridge: Cambridge University Press, 1994.

Bulman, Stephen. "A School for Epic? The 'Ecole William Ponty' and the Evolution of the Sunjata Epic, 1913–c. 1960." In *Epic Adventures: Heroic Narrative in the Oral Performance Traditions of Four Continents,* edited by Jan Jansen and Henk M. J. Maier, 34–45. Mûnster, Germany: Lit Verlag, 2004.

———. "The Buffalo-Woman Tale: Political Imperatives and Narrative Constraints in the Sunjata Epic." In *Discourse and Its Disguises: The Interpretation of African Oral Texts,* edited by Karin Barber and P. F. de Moraes Farias, 171–88. Birmingham, UK: Centre of West African Studies, University of Birmingham, 1989.

Camara, Laye. *The Guardian of the Word.* Translated by James Kirkup. New York:Vintage Books, 1984 (first Eng. tr. 1980, Fr. ed. *Kouma Lafôlô Kouma,* 1978).

Charry, Eric. *Mande Music: Traditional and Modern Music of the Maninka and Mandinka of Western Africa.* Chicago and London: University of Chicago Press, 2000.

Colleyn, Jean-Paul, ed. *Bamana: The Art of Existence in Mali.* New York: Museum for African Art, 2001.

Conrad, David C. "From the *banan* Tree of Kouroussa: Mapping the Landscape in Mande Traditional History." *Canadian Journal of African Studies* 42, 2–3 (2008): 384–408.

————. "Oral Tradition and Perceptions of History from the Manding Peoples of West Africa" in *Themes in West Africa's History* (ed. Emmanuel Kwaku Akeampong): 73–96. Athens OH: Ohio University Press, 2006.

————. "Mooning Armies and Mothering Heroes: Female Power in Mande Epic Tradition." In *In Search of Sunjata: The Mande Epic as History, Literature, and Performance,* edited by Ralph A. Austen, 89–229. Bloomington and Indianapolis: Indiana University Press, 1999a.

————, ed. *Epic Ancestors of the Sunjata Era: Oral Tradition from the Maninka of Guinea.* Madison, WI: African Studies Program, University of Wisconsin, 1999b.

————. "A Town Called Dakajalan: The Sunjata Tradition and the Question of Ancient Mali's Capital." *Journal of African History* 35 (1994): 355–77.

————. "Searching for History in the Sunjata Epic: The Case of Fakoli." *History in Africa* 19 (1992): 147–200.

————. "Islam in the Oral Traditions of Mali: Bilali and Surakata." *Journal of African History* 26 (1985): 33–49.

Conrad, David C., and Barbara E. Frank, eds. *Status and Identity in West Africa: Nyamakalaw of Mande.* Bloomington and Indianapolis: Indiana University Press, 1995.

Gibb, H. A. R., and J. H. Kramers. *Shorter Encyclopedia of Islam.* Ithaca: Cornell University Press, 1965.

Hale, Thomas A. *Griots and Griottes: Masters of Words and Music.* Bloomington and Indianapolis: Indiana University Press, 1998.

Hoffman, Barbara G. *Griots at War: Conflict, Conciliation, and Caste in Mande.* Bloomington and Indianapolis: Indiana University Press, 2000.

Innes, Gordon, ed. *Sunjata: Three Mandinka Versions*. London: School of Oriental and African Studies, University of London, 1974.

Jansen, Jan, and Clemens Zobel, eds. *The Younger Brother in Mande: Kinship and Politics in West Africa*. Leiden, The Netherlands: Research School CNWS, 1996.

Janson, Marloes. "The Narration of the Sunjata Epic as a Gendered Activity." In *Epic Adventures: Heroic Narrative in the Oral Performance Traditions of Four Continents*, edited by Jan Jansen and Henk M. J. Maier, 81–88. Münster, Germany: Lit Verlag, 2004.

———. *The Best Hand is the Hand That Always Gives: Griottes and their Profession in Eastern Gambia*. Leiden, The Netherlands: Research School CNWS, 2002.

Johnson, John William, ed. *Son-Jara: The Mande Epic*. 3rd ed. Text by Fa-Digi Sisòkò. Bloomington and Indianapolis: Indiana University Press, 2003.

Johnson, John William, Thomas A. Hale, and Stephen Belcher, eds. *Oral Epics from Africa: Vibrant Voices from a Vast Continent*. Bloomington and Indianapolis: Indiana University Press, 1997.

Koné, Kassim. "When Male Becomes Female and Female Becomes Male in Mande." *Mande Studies* 4 (2002): 21–29.

Levtzion, Nehemia. *Ancient Ghana and Mali*. London: Methuen & Co., 1973.

Levtzion, Nehemia, and J.F.P. Hopkins, eds. *Corpus of Early Arabic Sources for West African History*. Cambridge: Cambridge University Press, 1981.

Levtzion, Nehemia, and Jay Spaulding, eds. *Medieval West Africa: Views from Arab Scholars and Merchants*. Princeton, NJ: Markus Wiener Publishers, 2003.

McIntosh, Roderick J. *The Peoples of the Middle Niger: The Island of Gold*. Malden, MA and Oxford: Blackwell Publishers, Ltd., 1998.

McNaughton, Patrick R. *The Mande Blacksmiths: Knowledge, Power, and Art in West Africa.* Bloomington and Indianapolis: Indiana University Press, 1988.

Niane, Djibril Tamsir. *Sundiata: An Epic of Old Mali.* Translated by G. D. Pickett. London: Longman, 1965.

Suso, Bamba. *Sunjata,* edited by Graham Furniss and Lucy Duran. London and New York: Penguin Books, 2000.

Vansina, Jan. *Oral Tradition as History.* Madison, WI: The University of Wisconsin Press, 1985.